ALSO BY STEPHEN P. BARRY

Royal Service

Royal Secrets

ROYAL SECRETS

The View From Downstairs

STEPHEN P. BARRY

Villard Books
New York 1985

Library of Congress Cataloging in Publication Data
Barry, Stephen P., 1948–
Royal secrets.
Sequel to: Royal service.
1. Elizabeth II, Queen of Great Britain, 1926– —Family.
2. Great Britain—Kings and rulers—Biography.
3. Great Britain—Princes and princesses—Biography.
4. Great Britain—Royal household.
5. Barry, Stephen P., 1948–
6. Valets—Great Britain—Biography.
I. Title.
DA590.B   1985   941.085'092'2 [B]   84-40604
ISBN 0-394-54403-X

Preface

When I sat down to write my first book, *Royal Service*, in the spring of 1982, I had just ended my twelve-year employment as valet to the Prince of Wales. I had resigned six months previously, having decided to leave his service a few months after the Royal wedding in July 1981.

Looking back, in those first weeks of recalling life as it had been at Buckingham Palace, I understood why the years spent there did not seem so extraordinary. Since I had been in Royal employment from the age of eighteen until I was thirty-two, the Prince's way of life had, to a great extent, become my own. I had traveled the world with him, mostly living in luxury. I had learned from him how to enjoy the better things of life, inevitably had seen history being made from the inside, and had met many remarkable people on the way.

My life had been enhanced, but, in my turn, I had always done my best to make the Prince's life smooth. I helped him and Lady Diana keep their secrets in the early stages of their courtship. I helped him prepare for his wedding. I had even gone on his honeymoon with him and his charming bride, Diana, Princess of Wales. At the time I took it all for granted.

Today it hardly seems possible. At first, living in the real world was not easy. I had become accustomed to the rarefied atmosphere of Royalty. I had a lot of adjusting to do.

It was only as the months away from the Palace slipped by, and when my book came out in April of 1983, that I realized I had more to say, and that I could give a much broader insight into the subject of life with the Monarchy. Not only was I beginning to understand how enormously privileged I had been, but I was realizing that I had been given a place and a part in the cast of what I can only describe as the greatest show on earth.

I was also receiving many letters and being asked endless questions about how the Monarchy is run. People were curious about things that I had always taken completely for granted. What is an equerry? they wanted to know. What does a page do? Even, what does the Prince eat for breakfast? In spite of endless media coverage of Royalty, it became clear that only someone like myself, who had lived on the inside, could really give the answers to this insatiable quest for information.

People, I discovered, were fascinated not only by the great wealth and incomparable lifestyle of the Royal Family but by the trivia as well. I had all of that knowledge; I had been acquiring it unconsciously since I was eighteen years old.

Life behind the walls of the palaces and great houses where the Royal Family live out their lives is curiously sheltered and safe. But people who dwell in palaces are all interdependent on one another. And now I realize that, apart from their immediate family, members of Royalty are closer to those who serve them than to anyone else.

They were as dependent on us as we were on them.

We Royal servants instinctively learn to live by two Victorian adages, but with a different twist: it is not the children who should be seen but not heard—it is the servants. Conversely, in Royal homes, "not in front of the servants" rarely applies. Willy-nilly, the servants are always there, on hand, unobtrusive, but seeing and hearing all. Whatever happens in Royal circles—triumph or tragedy—always takes place in the presence of servants.

So this book is about what the page, the footman, the butler, the valet, the dresser, the housemaid, the policeman, the nanny, and the chef saw. And heard. It is also an affectionate record of life on both sides of the green baize doors and particularly in the areas of the Palace that were ours and where, once grown up, Royalty rarely ventured.

Royal history and customs, as learned by those of us who have been closest to the Royals in their service, are a large part of the story. *Royal Secrets* presents a special side of history—as told by the Royals themselves, and handed on down by the men and women who spend a lifetime with them, being seen and not heard.

I have lived in the Royal shadow and have enjoyed a carefully and delicately conducted friendship with the future King. Not a friendship in the ultimate sense; that would never be possible. Even today a Royal servant must always remember his or her place.

People from other lands are often amazed that British Royalty continues to be so strong in a rapidly changing world. I hope that this book will give an inkling of the reasons why.

Stephen Barry
Los Angeles, May 1984

Contents

CONTENTS

To my family,
for all their support

Upstairs

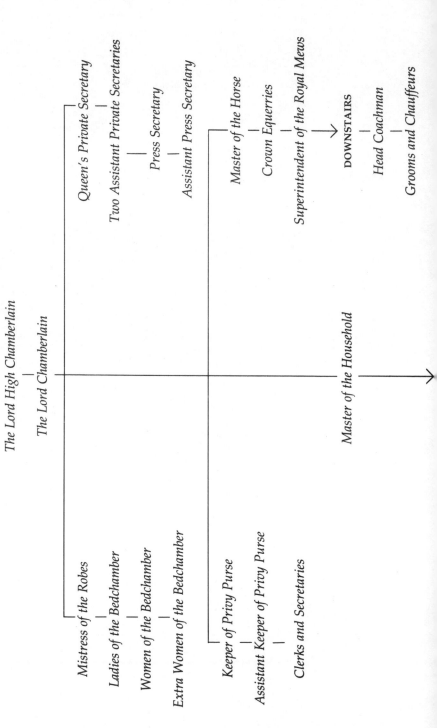

The Lord High Chamberlain

The Lord Chamberlain

Mistress of the Robes
Ladies of the Bedchamber
Women of the Bedchamber
Extra Women of the Bedchamber

Keeper of Privy Purse
Assistant Keeper of Privy Purse

Clerks and Secretaries

Queen's Private Secretary
Two Assistant Private Secretaries

Press Secretary

Assistant Press Secretary

Master of the Horse
Crown Equerries

Superintendent of the Royal Mews

Master of the Household

DOWNSTAIRS

Head Coachman

Grooms and Chauffeurs

Downstairs

Special Case:

Royal Dressers

GENERAL ———— *(Master of the Household)* ———— HOUSEKEEPING ———— FOOD

Palace Steward (Queen's Dresser)   *Head Housekeeper*   *Chef*

Deputy Palace Steward and Royal Valets   *Four Housekeepers for Royal Homes*   *Deputy Chef*

Four Pages of the Back Stairs   *Royal Nannies*

Four Yeomen   *Twenty-four Housemaids*

Four Pages of the Presence   *Daily Help*

Sergeant-Footman

Deputy Sergeant-Footman   *Kitchen*   *Pastry*

Two Queen's Footmen   *Twenty-two Staff and Porters*   *Three Staff and Porters*

Twelve Household Footmen

Under-Butlers (Pantries)

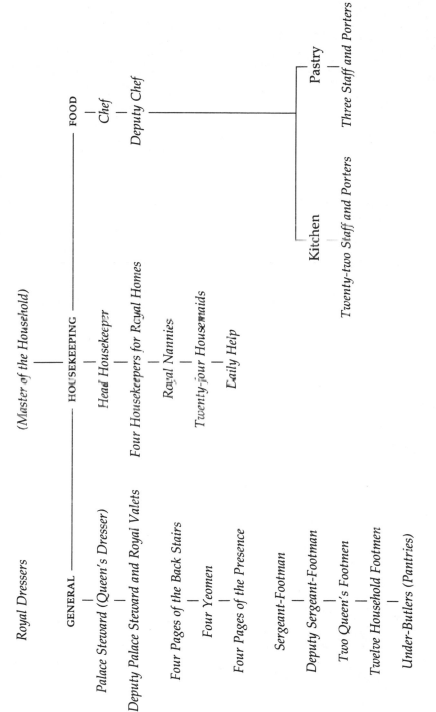

Royal Secrets

Chapter One

ALL THE QUEEN'S MEN

WHEREVER THE QUEEN IS, A MEMBER OF HER STAFF WILL BE either at hand or within calling distance. The Queen could never be said to be alone. And she sees more of those who are paid to be her personal attendants than of practically anyone else. That includes her husband, Prince Philip, the Duke of Edinburgh.

This is also true of Prince Charles, Princess Diana, and all the other top Royals. From the day those born Royal arrive on this earth, they are surrounded by servants—indeed, are brought up by them.

It seems crazy in retrospect, but I can remember occasions at Balmoral, the Royal summer holiday home in Scotland, when there would be one hundred and twenty members of staff looking after only six of the family. At those times we were barely occupied, though we would be working our socks off once the houseguests arrived.

The actual number of people the Queen employs has probably never been counted. A precise total would be difficult, considering the maintenance of her huge estates, Balmoral and Sandringham, and all the houses and farms that go with them. These she owns. Windsor Castle and Buckingham Palace she does not. The Duke of Edinburgh always says of Buckingham Palace, "It isn't ours. It's a tied cottage. We live over the shop."

From a financial point of view they probably thank their lucky stars every day that it *is* a "tied cottage." The Palace is owned and run by the nation, and it takes more than three hundred people to keep it going. Although it is the Queen's London home, it is more like a big office block—the headquarters of what Prince Philip calls "the firm."

The sole purpose of all Royal servants, senior and junior, is to ensure that the Queen's entire life runs smoothly. Hiccups and problems have to be hidden from her; nothing must ever be seen to go wrong. The end result is that the Royal Family never have to lift a finger on their own behalf —unless, of course, they do it for fun, and as a change from being waited on hand, foot, and finger, day and night.

Imagine: Barry Lovell, the Duke of Edinburgh's valet, has a task that he performs every night before he and his master retire. Barry is charged with placing the toothpaste ready on Prince Philip's toothbrush before His Royal Highness cleans his teeth at bedtime. And Barry has done this for so long now, as his predecessor did before him, that it doesn't even strike him as unusual.

One particular incident sums up the Royal attitude to service, and it concerns the Queen's uncle, the late Duke of Gloucester, who died in 1974. He was sitting by the fire at his home, Barnwell Manor, reading his paper, when a blazing log fell into the hearth. The Duke took not the slightest bit of notice, though the log was singeing the carpet and making a great deal of smoke.

Fortunately, a passing footman saw smoke edging its way under the door, and rushed in. Seeing what had happened, he grabbed the tongs and put the log back on the fire.

"About time, too," grunted the Duke, without even looking up from his paper.

The Royals don't like to use the word "servant." They feel it sounds demeaning to those who serve them. Also, the Queen is extremely conscious of the Royal image. She does not like to appear grand or extravagant, either of which she believes could cause British Royalty to lose popularity with her subjects all over the world.

This was vividly illustrated when, in an unprecedented move, the Palace called a press conference for the editors of all the national newspapers in 1981. The purpose—to ask the press not to hound Princess Diana night and day as, indeed, journalists from all over the world were doing at that time.

One of the Palace's complaints was that the Princess could not even pop into a sweetshop near her country home to buy her favorite winegums without being harassed and photographed. After Michael Shea, the Queen's Press Secretary, had put the Palace viewpoint to the editors, the Queen joined the group to talk to them herself, again an unprecedented move.

An editor from one of Britain's more sensational weeklies, who was mysteriously sporting a black eye, asked the Queen, "Why can't the Princess send a servant for her winegums?"

"That," said the Queen as she moved smartly away from him, "is one of the most pompous remarks I have ever heard."

Pompous the Royals are not. Grand—yes, though not particularly extravagant, considering the vast fortunes that some of them control. There is certainly no family in the world with the same lifestyle—no one could begin to match the way they live—which, incidentally, they take for granted.

Most of the people in Royal service will see the Queen once a year. Others are deeply involved in her private life and the private lives of her family—and have been for many years. I was fortunate enough to be one of the involved ones for the twelve years that I was valet to Prince Charles. For fifteen years I was a Royal servant, starting as an eighteen-year-old footman, falling into the category known as "Staff."

When I became Prince Charles's valet, I was still Staff, the lowliest of the three levels of Royal household. Top of the pile are the Household, and in the middle are the Officials, all three levels making up about three hundred and fifty people, plus part-time extra staff.

The members of the Household are courtiers, most of them close friends of the Royal Family. There are around thirty of these actually working in the Palace on a day-to-day basis. There are also three Equerries, each one a serving officer from the three armed forces. In the past, an Equerry's job was to ride beside the King's or Queen's carriage to protect the Monarch. Today, the position is more ceremonial. Whenever the Queen inspects one of her armed forces the Equerry from that service will be the traditional two paces behind.

One of these men is always on duty. They live in the Palace, and even accompany the Queen on private holidays. Their role then involves greeting guests and generally overseeing the staff on the Queen's behalf.

The second category, the Officials and Clerks, act as secretaries and office workers under the direction of members of the Household. There are at least a hundred men and women in this group who work full-time. When an important ceremonial event such as the Royal wedding takes place, many more are brought in on a temporary basis to deal with invitations and all the extra work that such an occasion entails.

Last (but certainly not least) are the Staff, who maintain a very strict pecking order among themselves. Twenty-four of these hold senior positions, controlling another nearly one hundred and twenty people. Most members of this group wear uniform or livery of some kind. Another large section of Staff works at the back of the Palace in the Royal Mews. They have their own order of precedence and are under the control of the Crown Equerry, who ranks much higher than the ordinary Equerries.

The Household—capital *T* and *H*—are the upper crust of the Royal servants: people fulfilling positive jobs who still retain their archaic titles. The people who hold these top-echelon positions are mostly of the aristocracy, rich in their own right. They form an enclave of the mysterious body of those with power and influence who are known in Britain as the Establishment.

No one in Britain could just reel off the names of the members of the Establishment, but their effect on life in that country is considerable. And the Queen's Household are very much part of this undercover group of people.

Although money in Britain has shifted to industrialists and tycoons, those who form the Queen's Household are still, in the main, enormously wealthy. When they leave one of the Queen's palaces or castles, they go home to their own.

The McClean of McClean, the chief of the Scottish Clan McClean who for many years was the Queen's Lord Chamberlain, has now retired to his ancestral home, Duart Castle in Scotland. This superb ancient pile is fairly typical of the lifestyle of most of the Queen's close friends who head the Household. Duart Castle is enormous, located on an island, and richly furnished.

The less affluent members of the Household, such as widowed ladies-in-waiting or retired clergy who have served the Queen personally, will live in grace-and-favor residences—

apartments or houses provided by the Queen, which are usually part of the complex of either Saint James's Palace, Windsor Castle, or Hampton Court Palace.

The Queen's new Lord Chamberlain, Lord Airlie (brother-in-law to Princess Alexandra), is responsible for the overall running of the Court. In modern terms he is the top administrator, or managing director, in charge of all the Queen's men. An archaic hangover from the past was his power to censor all live theater in the United Kingdom, but this privilege was abolished in 1967. Today one of his duties which remains from earlier times is to arrange most State occasions. His last big production was Prince Charles and Lady Diana's wedding.

Her Lord Steward is the Duke of Northumberland, whose family has played a part in British history from the days of the Plantagenet Kings. His role is entirely ceremonial, and carries no salary. In fact, he is rarely seen at the Palace. He will leave his castle in Northumberland or his stately home, Syon Park near West London, only to put in an appearance at a great State occasion. In the past the Lord Steward was in charge of the Monarch's food and attended the King at meals. Now the only concession to the past is that on State occasions he wears a Household black tailcoat, black breeches and black silk stockings, buckled shoes and white bow tie. Topped, of course, by his medals and decorations.

What once were the main duties of the Lord Steward have now been taken over by the Master of the Household, currently Sir Peter Ashmore. He is comptroller of all indoor staff at the Palace. Sir Peter was a vice admiral in the Royal Navy, and his appointment constitutes something of a break with tradition. In the recent past, the Master of the Household came from the army, usually from one of the crack guards regiments.

The Queen's Private Secretary, Sir Philip Moore, is the one member of the Household who will see the Queen every day. His role is to act as the link between the Queen and the

Prime Minister. All Government papers are routed through him. He is the Queen's principal political adviser, and he accompanies her on all Royal tours as her official ears and eyes. An extremely pleasant man, he comes from an Indian Civil Service background and now lives close at hand in all the Royal residences. Two Assistant Private Secretaries deputize in his absence and control a battery of officials and clerks. He is also in charge of the Press Office.

The top lady-in-waiting, known as the Mistress of the Robes, is the Duchess of Grafton. A close friend of the Queen's, she will be in attendance standing behind the Monarch at the State openings of Parliament, and other occasions. The title originally went with the task of caring for the Queen's robes. Today this is performed by the Queen's Dressers, who are, of course, Staff.

Under the Mistress of the Robes are the Ladies of the Bedchamber. Marchionesses and Countesses, mostly part-time, they attend the Queen on lesser State occasions. As these are the Queen's personal friends, there are no set limits to their number.

The Women of the Bedchamber are also chosen from her friends, but there are only four of them, who work on a rotating basis. Like the duty Equerry, one of them will always be with the Queen; in fact, they could be described as a female equivalent of the Equerry.

Both the Ladies and Women of the Bedchamber are more commonly known as ladies-in-waiting. All Royal women have at least two of these always on duty. Princess Diana has two, neither of whom is her own age, which is a pity. Princess Margaret has six, sometimes eight. The Queen Mother, like the Queen, may have as many as she wishes. The Golden Rule for ladies-in-waiting is never to be better dressed than your Royal mistress.

At functions, Royal ladies are always given flowers, usually by children. Sometimes it is a spontaneous gesture of a posy, sometimes a formally presented bouquet. Princess

Diana gets a lot of the spontaneous kind. After the flowers have been received, they are held for a moment and then passed to the lady-in-waiting. By the end of a particularly long walkabout, the lady-in-waiting looks like a flower-stall —unless she can manage to pass some on to one of the accompanying policemen, who would really rather not take them, on the ground of security and their need for free hands. It makes a good excuse.

Again, the ladies-in-waiting are generally titled or, if not, certainly well-connected and, more important, rich. They need to be because, though they are paid expenses and helped with their clothing for special occasions, theirs are honorary positions.

Another prominent figurehead is the Master of the Horse, the Earl of Westmoreland. He is the man seen at the side of the Queen as she rides down the Mall every June on her official birthday. He disappears into the background for the Trooping of the Color Ceremony that follows the ride. On this occasion the Queen wears the uniform of one of her crack guards regiments, and her Master of the Horse wears his scarlet uniform with plumed hat. The job is not demanding. The Earl and his wife are among the Queen's closest personal friends, spending holidays with the Royal Family. The Master of the Horse is officially in charge of the Royal Mews, although the day-to-day running of this section of the Queen's residences is done by the Crown Equerry.

The Royal Mews, set in a corner of Buckingham Palace gardens, used to be the home exclusively of the King's horses and carriages. Today they also provide shelter for the Queen's automobiles, the six State Rolls-Royces, plus the twenty or so cars used by the Household. Garaged there are the Royal Family's personal cars, too, including Prince Charles's old Aston Martin, and Prince Philip's Range Rover.

The State coaches are kept in the Mews as well, along with the various smaller carriages. These can be seen quite often in London when the Queen is receiving new ambassadors. She always sends a carriage, usually drawn by at least four horses, to bring them to the Palace.

With twelve horses in residence at any time, the Mews is a corner of London that still smells of the country. In fact, it resembles a village. Above the stables are many apartments, occupied by the Coachman, the Postilions (the men who ride the horses pulling the carriages), the Royal Chauffeurs, and not forgetting the Royal Blacksmith. The Crown Equerry has a very fine house there, at the entrance to the Mews.

Twice a week this little "village" is open to the public. It is the only part of the Palace grounds that is easily accessible, which means that security is always very much on the Royal Equerry's mind.

Over the years while I worked at the Palace there was some attempt to make the Household a little more democratic. But the "Old Boy network" has lost little power, though one could give full marks to Prince Philip, in particular, for trying to make alterations. Nothing much has changed. The old order hangs in there, jealously guarding its privileges.

Take one simple example: under no circumstances can anyone who has been in Her Majesty's armed forces and then come into Royal service become a private secretary unless he formerly held a commission. There is no chance for a private or noncommissioned officer, however brilliant. This rule does not apply to an applicant who has never been in the armed forces. These rules remain hidebound and archaic.

The middle level of Royal workers, the Officials—the accountants, secretaries, and clerks—are the nine-to-five people. Staff and Officials don't get on. They have a healthy dislike of each other. Officials, who rarely set eyes on real live Royals, are jealous of Staff's proximity to them. And Staff can't bear Officials' superior attitudes.

Still, these middle-echelon people are efficient. Mostly

faceless and working behind the scenes, some will eventually receive those honors that are given only at the Monarch's own behest. At the end of their service they may see their names on the New Year or Birthday Honors Lists. They then present themselves before the Queen at an investiture where she will personally award them, either with a medal or an insignia, or, if they're very lucky, with a title.

From then on, they are entitled to use after their names the initials of whichever order they have been given. Or, of course, the title, if that has been their reward. Financially, it means nothing. The honor is all.

But not for everyone. A break with tradition came when the Queen honored her detective, Commander Albert Perkins, with a knighthood on his retirement. It was not a particularly popular appointment at the Palace, as most of us weren't crazy about Albert. When he became Sir Albert, it was something of a surprise, as he was the first ordinary policeman to be given a bona fide title.

Some weeks after the investiture, one of the Household met Albert's wife coming out of one of Britain's biggest supermarkets, carrying her own groceries.

"Good morning, Lady Perkins," he said, raising his hat.

She looked around with a hunted expression, hoping no one had heard. "Shh!" she said, finger to lips. "Isn't it silly!"

She was probably right. In 1984, maybe titles are silly. But in Britain many people—actors, industrialists, politicians— go to extraordinary lengths hoping to get themselves what is colloquially known as a "handle."

The bottom rung of the ladder—Staff—is where the characters are. Top of the Staff pecking order is Cyril Dickman, the Palace Steward. Over thirty-three years ago he went to work at Clarence House as a footman for the young Princess Elizabeth. By the time I came to the Palace, he was already moving up the ladder, and I watched his progress from page to Palace Steward. Today, in his fifties, he holds the top job in Staff. But he is not, and never will be, considered a member of the exalted Household, because he is an ordinary, affable, below-stairs chap who made it.

Cyril is assisted by a Deputy Palace Steward, who shares equal rank with the Royal Valets and Dressers, followed by the Pages of the Back Stairs, the Monarch's personal pages. The ancient title comes from the days when their duty was to guide the King's mistresses (or the Queen's lovers) up the back stairs—and keep their mouths shut about it afterwards. Obviously, the Pages of the Back Stairs were highly trusted, as they are even today—though for quite different reasons, let me say hastily.

The Queen and Prince Philip each has two of these pages, one on duty while the other is off. These four men control access to their employers. One of the anachronisms of the Monarchy is that pages confirm all the private engagements of the Queen and Prince Philip. Even the private secretaries have to go through them to gain access to the Royal apartments. In theory, the system gives the pages a lot of power; they could wield considerable influence, excluding those they don't want their employers to see. This has the effect of sometimes making members of the Household extremely suspicious that their way is deliberately being blocked.

Prince Charles does not have a page, so I fulfilled the role for him while I was his valet. Despite the grumbles of the private secretaries at having to deal with the pages, I found that the system works to the advantage of Royalty. If the Prince did not want to see someone or to keep an engagement, I was the one who told the lies, made the excuses, saying that he was otherwise engaged or, simply, that I couldn't find him anywhere.

There are only a few private rooms in the Palace, which are the sole places where a member of the family can seek sanctuary and talk to relatives or to close friends. Anyone other than family had to make an appointment to see the Prince. Through me.

However, two people were exceptions to this custom:

Lady Susan Hussey, the Queen's lady-in-waiting, and the Prince's former nanny, Mabel Anderson, the only person outside his family who calls him Charles. It seems extraordinary, but even Lady Diana called him "sir" until they were engaged. After the engagement, she successfully managed to avoid calling him anything. Now she calls him Charles— or, more often, "darling."

One day Lady Susan Hussey was having tea with the Prince when Squadron Leader David Checketts, Private Secretary to the Prince, buzzed me from his office downstairs to ask if the Prince was around.

"I'm sorry," I said, "he's engaged at the moment with Lady Susan."

"Oh, hell!" he said.

Later, he wandered up and, pointing to the Prince's closed door, asked, "Who's in there?"

When I said it was Nanny Mabel, who had popped in close on the heels of Lady Susan, he exploded. "Why is my life constantly obstructed by ladies-in-waiting and bloody nannies!" he bawled.

The Prince and his secretary had many differences. From the sidelines I could see it was just a matter of temperaments. David Checketts had been appointed by Prince Philip to watch over Prince Charles when he attended Geelong, the outback Australian school. Checketts was much older than the Prince; he had been an air force service Equerry, and had originally worked for the Duke. He did rather play the heavy father with Prince Charles.

In desperation the Prince went to see Great-uncle Dickie —Lord Mountbatten. The regimen was too oppressive, he complained.

He told me that Lord Mountbatten had said, "Get rid of him, but give him a title and he'll be perfectly happy."

Which is exactly what happened. The Squadron Leader became Sir David Checketts, and all was settled amicably.

At that time I was acting as a page. By tradition, only the

top Royals—the Queen, the Queen Mother, and Prince Philip—have them. For the time being, Prince Charles had the next best thing, a butler. In fact, though they won't thank me for saying so, all Palace pages are basically glorified butlers.

They don't do a lot. They have their dignity to consider, dressed as they are on State occasions in black tailcoats, beige knee-breeches, and white stockings. They serve the Queen at table, they introduce and present people, and they act as ushers.

People imagine pages will be young boys. Those known as the Queen's Pages of Honor are. These are the sons of nobility, whose only role in the pageant of Monarchy is to carry the Queen's train at the opening of Parliament, or at any time when she wears the crown and the robes. Usually four boys are appointed, but it is not a job for life; they retire at sixteen.

Following the Pages of the Back Stairs in Staff protocol are the Queen's four Yeomen. These men rarely see the Queen. But they head the four sections that run her domestic life.

The Yeoman of the Plate looks after all the Queen's gold and silver plate and cutlery. This must be the finest in the world, and it is used on the grandest of State occasions. The six members of the Yeoman's staff are called under-butlers, and their duty is to care for this amazing treasure trove. The hundreds of plates, candlesticks, table centers are housed deep in the Palace, wrapped in airtight bags, and counted after every use.

The task of the Yeoman of the Glass and China is to oversee the setting of the tables on great occasions. He has a staff of four, and they care for the fabulous china and crystal that the Monarch owns. There are hundreds and hundreds of glasses, and bone china services, all kept in various cabinets around the Palace and gathered up when needed. Everything is still carefully washed and dried by hand.

Although the Royal Family drink very little, the Queen

still employs a Yeoman of the Wine Cellars. The wine cellars are below the basement and are kept at a carefully controlled temperature. He also orders thousands of bottles of spirits and soft drinks each year for the endless stream of guests who come to the Palace. He has staff of two cellar men.

A fairly recent appointment is the Traveling Yeoman, who takes care of all the Queen's traveling arrangements, both in England and abroad. He will make a reconnaissance trip with others of her staff—usually her private secretary and security man—booking hotel rooms and generally seeing the world in privileged circumstances. He is also responsible for moving the Queen's large staff around the Royal residences.

Though the other Yeomen normally stay with the Court, sometimes they too get to travel. If the Queen, on a State visit to another country, gives a State banquet, she takes along her own gold plate, her own candelabra, her own china and sometimes her own wines. With them she takes the three Yeomen, turning the British Embassy into a home away from home.

These Yeomen, incidentally, are not to be confused with the Yeomen of the Guard at the Tower of London, commonly known as "Beefeaters." The Tower Yeomen are quasi-soldiers, permanently on sentry duty, while the Palace Yeomen are senior Royal Staff.

Not quite so senior are the Pages of the Presence, a less grand category of page than those of the Back Stairs. They are controlled by the Deputy Palace Steward, who has another title as well. He is also called the Groom of the Chambers.

The four Pages of the Presence look after the Household and Household meals, and also act as ushers and guides at formal State occasions. At investitures they come into their own. Then the Palace is swarming with pages to guide the hundred and fifty or so of Her Majesty's subjects who have come down the Mall to be honored in some way.

When the Queen is knighting someone, it is the job of a

Page of the Back Stairs to hold the sword, which he then hands to the Queen's Equerry, who in turn hands it to her. She uses it to tap gently on both shoulders of the person who is being knighted. Contrary to popular belief, she does not say, "Arise, Sir . . . " She will say a few words of congratulation, having been briefed on the background of her subject whom she is ennobling.

While all this is going on, another Page of the Back Stairs is holding the Queen's purse. You will never see the Queen without her purse, even though there is not a great deal in it. Certainly no money.

When I say that odd characters are in Staff, it is true. One of them for many years was Ernest Bennett, the Queen's Page. After thirty years of service he has now retired, and lives in a grace-and-favor residence at Kensington Palace. When an extra hand is needed around the Palace, he still comes to help.

Bennett held the Queen's purse for many years. He worked for her while she was still Princess Elizabeth and a young bride, living at Clarence House (where the Queen Mother now lives). He moved with the Queen to the Palace after her father died.

Ernest Bennett is considered to be almost family. He can reel off the names of the Queen's many godchildren. He knows the family history as well as they do. He is a prime source of stories, as he goes back to the days of old Queen Mary; he worked for her brother, the Duke of Athlone, before he went into the Queen's service, and was very fond of Queen Mary.

During the war, the Kensington Palace apartment of Princess Alice, Countess of Athlone (Queen Mary's sister-in-law), had been damaged. Queen Mary insisted on helping with the cleaning up, and she and Ernest Bennett worked in the kitchen together, washing the dust off the bone china. He washed; she wiped.

"She was very good," he said approvingly. "She didn't

actually dry the china, she patted it. Mind you, it took all afternoon to wash a dinner service!"

It's not surprising that he can—and does—get away with murder with the Queen.

If she is giving a large party, the Queen will receive guests at the top of the grand staircase, leading into the Picture Gallery. This in turn leads to the Ballroom. Those being received walk up this magnificent flight of stairs, to find the Queen and the Duke of Edinburgh waiting for them, flanked by the gentlemen of the Household. Standing behind her will be her Page of the Back Stairs—frequently Bennett, come to fill a vacancy.

Most of those presented will know Bennett of old. After they have been greeted by the Queen and have shaken her hand, they pass on and begin to chat and gossip with her ex-page, wanting to know how he is. Often the line will be held up while Bennett exchanges news. The Queen never seems to mind but, then, she herself loves gossip.

We had a Palace joke that the only time Her Majesty was free of gossip was when she took her corgis for a walk. The rest of the time someone or other from Staff would be feeding her bits of information about what was going on in the Palace.

Bennett was always great for a chat and a bit of news. He'd trap the Queen in her sitting room with the latest; if she went through to her bedroom, her dresser "Bobo" McDonald would be waiting there with more information. I doubt if anything happens in any of her many homes that doesn't get back to the Queen in double-quick time.

I remember, some years ago, a bemused young footman who had gone into the Bow Room at Buckingham Palace to collect his Christmas gift from her. It was his last week of Royal service. He had decided that the life was not for him, and had handed in his resignation to the Palace Steward. There are twelve footmen working at the Palace at all times, and the Queen probably never lays eyes on most of them. She most certainly would not know all their names.

Just the same, she said, "I hear you are moving on, John."

"Yes, Your Majesty," he said, startled.

"Ah, well. Happy New Year," she said drily, handing over the gift-wrapped pair of woolen socks.

"Now, how the hell did she know I was going?" he asked afterwards. The answer undoubtedly was that either Bennett or Bobo, or one of her own two personal footmen, had passed on the information. The Queen Mother will have no part of staff gossip. Nor will Prince Philip; but, then, both their lives are much less restricted than the Queen's.

The Pages of the Back Stairs and the Pages of the Presence do get most of the interesting things to do. For example, when President Reagan stayed at Windsor Castle as the Queen's guest, he and Mrs. Reagan were both appointed pages, as a courtesy to a visiting head of state. The Queen lent the President one of hers, and one of Prince Philip's was assigned to Mrs. Reagan. Behind the green baize door at Windsor, there was much amusement at the Secret Service men's faces when they saw these quaint fellows, in their black tailcoats and beige knee-breeches, helping to care for the President and his wife.

In this instance the pages would have had to liaise with the President's staff to make sure that nothing went wrong with any of the arrangements. It is a responsible job, as even a little slip-up—with the Queen standing tapping her foot in the hall somewhere, waiting for the President—would have marred the occasion. Or vice versa, come to that.

There was one tricky moment during the President's visit. The staff are all very well aware of the Queen's danger signals; we all know exactly when her temper is about to explode, and it is time to empty the room. Fast! When she is building into a highly controlled rage, the Queen twists her wedding ring on her finger and her mouth begins to move as if she is about to say something extremely positive.

The President might never have realized that he had incurred her displeasure on the morning of their famous ride in Windsor Great Park. There was the President in his cowboy gear, the Queen in her traditional riding-clothes, mounted on Burmese, the horse she had ridden at the Trooping of the Color the previous year when a youth in the crowd fired blanks at her. Also present were a great many reporters and photographers.

Now, the Queen might just bring herself to say "Good morning" to a press man—one she had come to know over the years—but light banter with journalists is not her style.

The President had turned their meeting at Windsor Castle into an impromptu press conference, and the Queen was furious. We could all see the mouth working and the wedding ring whizzing around, and we thought, "Hang onto your cowboy hat, Mr. President"—until she suddenly turned and rode away.

Afterwards, the Palace grapevine discovered that she had felt the President was using her for political purposes, and, like Queen Victoria, she was not amused. But, ever the diplomat, that night at dinner she smoothed over the situation, saying Burmese had been restless and she felt it was wiser to let him ride on.

The incident was hardly the pages' fault. As far as their duties were concerned, the occasion went off splendidly.

The Secret Service is not alone in its incredulity at grown men being called pages. Bennett tells a story about the time when he went with the Queen to Nigeria. Like all Royal tours, it had been planned months in advance, with accommodation booked for everyone and all arrangements made. Bennett was on the accommodation list as "E. Bennett, Page." When he arrived in his room, he discovered it was full of toys, and to add insult to injury, it was furnished with a child's bed, in which he was supposed to sleep. The Nigerians, like many others, were convinced that a page would be a small boy. They couldn't believe it when a man in his forties arrived.

"What did you do with the toys?" I asked him when he came home and was gleefully recounting the story in the canteen at the Palace.

"Brought them home for my son, of course," he said.

A friend of mine from Palace days who had wanted to be a page fell into this same trap when he applied for a job with the Queen.

"What are you doing now?" the Master of the Household asked him.

"I'm a page at the Dorchester Hotel," said John, aged sixteen.

"Ho-ho-ho," said the Master, finding this extremely funny. "You won't be one of those here."

Indeed he wasn't. They put him in the silver pantry, cleaning silver.

Another duty of the Pages of the Presence is to look after the very important guests who come to stay with the Queen. While I was working for Prince Charles, we started a new custom, at the Easter Court at Windsor, called Dine and Sleep. It meant that the Queen, who was technically on holiday and at home for the thirty-odd days of this Court, could invite people to dinner, give them a bed for the night, and say goodbye the next morning. It also meant that she could entertain a great many more people than when guests stayed for longer periods.

The guests arrive at about seven o'clock, to be met by an equerry or lady-in-waiting (according to sex), and are shown their rooms. After dressing, each guest is collected, generally by a page. But if it is someone very important, an equerry will act as escort when the guest is taken to the Green Drawing Room for drinks before dinner.

The guests are housed in the various towers that surround this vast medieval fortress that was modernized at enormous cost to the British by George IV early in his reign.

The biggest difficulty with important guests is that the page who is responsible for a particular tower of the castle has a problem finding out what they will want for breakfast. If he doesn't catch the V.I.P. before the equerry takes him or her off for dinner, the page has to wait up half the night for people to come to bed before he can pop the question. Of course, the problem does not exist if the page is escorting the guest to the drawing room. He just asks on the way.

They avoided this particular problem with the Right Honorable Edward Heath, then Prime Minister of Great Britain, when he came to dine and sleep. Edward Heath, who speaks with the strangled vowels that enrage real aristocracy, was considered a rather pompous man. He announced through the aide who accompanied him that he would like an egg for breakfast. Boiled for exactly four minutes.

It was an unwise choice. Windsor is the largest residential castle in the world; the enormous vaulted kitchens where breakfasts are cooked are probably half a mile away from the guest rooms. The Prime Minister's egg was duly boiled for four minutes, then kept warm while being delivered on a silver tray by a footman.

Not surprisingly, it was like a bullet. The Prime Minister sent it back.

Eventually the footman returned with another four-minute egg. Another bullet. Heath's breakfast was doomed to disaster. One of the footmen—who had to tramp those miles of corridors—was heard to mutter that a real gentleman would have eaten it anyway and not made such a fuss.

The footmen are characters too. To explain their function: I suppose Americans would call them "gofers." They run about doing everyone's will, dressed in red knee-breeches and black tailcoats with red waistcoats. The most senior is the Sergeant-Footman, who is answerable to the Queen herself. He has a deputy; between them, these two are in charge of the dozen or so men employed in this job. The Sergeant-Footman handles the staff's travel connections when the

Royal Family move in their stately, luggage-laden way from residence to residence. The trick is to ensure that the staff who are moving with them and dealing with the baggage get where they are supposed to be. And on time.

There are actually three classes of footman. There are eight ordinary ones, which is what I was when I first started in service at the Palace. All eight are usually on duty in the Palace at any time. Their main jobs are: to serve at table, act as valet for anyone who does not have one of his own, take the dogs for walks, run messages within the Palace, and ride as attendants outside carriages.

Then come Nursery Footmen; these don't exist at the moment, as the Palace nursery is no longer occupied, and Prince Charles is not yet grand enough to have them for Prince William and Prince Harry. I was Nursery Footman for a while, before I moved on to become the Prince of Wales's valet.

The Nursery Footman's time belonged to the Royal Nanny and the Royal children. My charges were Mabel Anderson and Prince Andrew and Prince Edward. At the time the children were young, Prince Edward being not much more than a baby. I didn't have to do any personal chores for the little Princes—that was Nanny Anderson's department—but I did have to run errands for her, bring her trays, and generally make myself useful. There was also a nursery maid to help.

One of my duties was to try to keep Prince Andrew amused. It was a formidable task, as he was a boisterous, active child who never seemed to settle for a moment. He always wanted to be where he wasn't allowed, and even at that age, he had a strong personality and was very good-looking. He had a habit of pulling the footman's tails—which often got him a slap when no one was looking. Happily for all of us who worked in the nursery, Prince Edward was a much quieter child.

In those days, on Mabel Anderson's nights off, the Queen

would come and baby-sit her children. Her own page and footman would attend her, so there was nothing for me to do. I always felt she enjoyed those quiet evenings with the sleeping children. The nursery quarters are out of use now. They have been turned into a flat for Prince Andrew.

The third rank of footman is the grandest. Called the Queen's Footmen, just two work directly for Her Majesty. This, of course, is the best job of all if you are a footman. And one of the ways to get there is if the corgis—all twelve of them—who patter around the Queen like you.

Some years ago one particular footman, Basil Stibbs, seemed to have it made. The corgis adored him. Whenever he entered Her Majesty's presence, the dogs would leave her feet and cluster around him, yapping their delight.

"You're so good with the dogs, Basil," the Queen would say.

"Yes, Your Majesty, I'm very fond of them," Basil would reply modestly.

"Come on, Basil," I said to him one day. "What's the secret?"

At first he protested that there wasn't one, but finally, looking around to see that no one was about, he fished in the pocket deep in the tail of his dresscoat.

And produced a lamb chop.

"I always keep one in there," he said in a confidential whisper. "Works a treat, doesn't it?"

Stories about the perfidies of staff are rife in the Palace.

One footman, determined to get the Beatles' autographs when they came to the Palace to receive their Member of the British Empire honor, "pinched" a sheet of Palace notepaper. As they were coming away from the investiture, he approached them.

"Excuse me," he said, "but Princess Anne is in the nursery and not able to come down. She would very much like your autographs. Would you please sign here?" He thrust the notepaper and a pen at them.

Meekly, they signed.

Footmen on the whole are an irreverent lot. One (who had better be nameless) calls the Queen and Prince Philip "Mother" and "Father" behind their backs. "Father's in a right old mood this morning," he'll say.

Another, who works for Princess Anne, always refers to her as "Anne Elizabeth Alice Louise"—her full name—when she has been a little on the grumpy side about something or another.

One of the footmen's least liked duties is riding on the back of the Royal coaches in cold or wet weather. Originally, of course, they were there to protect the occupants of the coach.

At Prince Charles's wedding to Lady Diana Spencer, the reality of the job, as opposed to the ceremonial, was restored. A not-so-plainclothes policeman, in breeches and a tricorn hat, "rode shotgun" as the open landau left the Palace for Waterloo Station, from where the Prince and Princess were leaving for their honeymoon. But in the policeman's red breeches was concealed a pistol, specially issued that morning from Cannon Row, the Scotland Yard police station responsible for guarding the Royal Family. Unlike the custom in other countries, policemen in Britain are normally not armed. Another policeman was fitted out exactly the same on the back of the Queen and Prince Philip's coach.

These policemen must have experienced something that is familiar to all footmen. When you ride on the back of the coaches, there are certain places—usually where the road is narrow—where every word the crowd says becomes audible.

I used to overhear remarks like "Oh look, there's Mum!" "She don't half look her age, don't she?" "Ain't she a blooming marvel?" as the Queen Mother was graciously nodding and bowing to the crowd. Or "Blimey, get a load of that hat!"—usually about Princess Anne, who has a rather odd taste in headgear. I can assure you from my own experience that while the crowd voices their opinions, the footmen have a hard time keeping a straight face. As indeed do the Royals, because what the footmen hear they hear too.

Footmen aren't the only perfidious ones. Many years ago a valet (called Jerome) ordered a whisky sent up every night for his master, King George VI, the present Queen's father. This became a regular routine. Until one night the whisky arrived when Jerome was off duty. The glass was solemnly handed to the King by one of his pages.

"What's this?" asked the King testily. "I never drink whisky."

Jerome did. But his nightcap ceased from then on.

The King *was* a testy man, according to those who worked for him. Only his wife, now the Queen Mother, could soothe him when he was in a bad mood. He had, according to his valet, one peculiar habit. He used to take out his frustrations on his bath sponge, squeezing and twisting it. In his day Royal sponges had a very short life.

Valets and dressers form part of the Staff section of Palace employees. These are rather privileged jobs, as there is so much contact with those for whom they work. Basically, the job involves looking after the Royals' enormous wardrobes. Prince Charles, for example, had forty-four uniforms alone, not counting his civilian clothes, and then there are all the ceremonial robes and gowns. These were all kept in a large room near his apartment.

A valet puts his master's clothes out ready in the morning, after having drawn the curtains and run the bath. He then discreetly leaves until sent for. A valet has to know which decorations go with which uniforms and must keep a close eye on his master's working schedule; the right clothes for an occasion must always be clean, pressed, and, if necessary, mended by the Palace seamstresses, well in time.

I used to buy most of Prince Charles's clothing, either by going out shopping for him, or by asking tailors, bootmakers, and so on to come to the Palace with cloth or leather patterns and then to return for fittings.

It's necessary to be able to pack in such a way that clothing comes out virtually uncreased and ready to wear. I also had to pack so that I knew exactly where each garment was. In that way the Prince could change, say on an aircraft, without my having to disrupt an entire suitcase. On overseas tours, I rarely unpacked. I would keep the clothes in open suitcases or hanging around the walls.

Taking care of laundry and dry cleaning was also my responsibility. I would wash his handkerchiefs myself, as otherwise they were always being stolen for souvenirs.

Another offbeat duty that valets are in charge of is tipping the staff at hotels, private houses, or embassies where Royalty stays. I carried a float of money from the Prince's office, and afterwards I would account for what I had spent. Royalty never carries money, which may explain why they appear to be so tight with it. I suppose to appreciate how much life costs these days, it is necessary to have a more personal sense of what money *won't* buy than they possibly can.

When I first went to the Palace, not only was the pay poor (it still isn't generous) but conditions were not particularly good. Today things have changed. There is even a small branch of the Civil Service trade union operating at the Palace. It is not very popular, as most of the servants feel it is disloyal to belong to it. But it has secured proper rates of pay.

As a footman at Windsor, I lived in what can only be described as a cubicle. Balmoral was worse. The footmen were—and still are—housed in temporary Nissen-type huts that were erected for the servants during the Czar of Russia's visit to Queen Victoria in 1882. The huts are still in use, but at least there are some heaters in them now.

A lot of the more primitive aspects of the job changed with the arrival of a new Master of the Household, Brigadier

Hardy Roberts, in 1969. He had been administrator of one of the big London hospitals, and is a very efficient man. The brigadier was appalled by much of what went on in Royal service. He started a system in which food and welfare meetings were conducted by the employees. Each section—the housemaids, the footmen, the chefs—nominates a representative to speak on its behalf. We used to sit in the billiards room (which isn't a billiards room at all, but just a place used for meetings) and say our pieces.

I found these little union-type gatherings not only a waste of time but highly comic. Everyone moaned and complained, usually about the food, which would make the representative from the kitchens bristle. On one occasion there was a steaming argument about the length of spaghetti! The housemaids were always wanting new plugs for their kettles, so that they could make their cups of tea. It was all silly and time-wasting, but if you didn't turn up, the Master wanted to know why.

I remember one footman requesting that there be a hobbies room for the staff at the Palace. This was looked on askance. "Well, can I keep a lathe in my room?" he asked. As most of the footmen were more into needlepoint than into metalwork, the macho Prince Philip, had he known about it, would have been delighted with this request. The Master, sensing approval from higher up, gave his.

Unfortunately, this particular footman had a passion for explosives. With another Palace employee, he had been robbing mines all around the country for sticks of gelignite, using a stolen vehicle to do so. It wouldn't have been found out, maybe, if he hadn't made the false number plates for his stolen Land-Rover on the lathe in the hobbies room and had the cheek to park the Land-Rover in the Palace forecourt.

At first, when the explosives were found on the Palace premises, there was a great scare and fear that the footmen were members of the IRA, the terrorist organization that killed Mountbatten. Happily, it turned out they were only bizarrely interested in explosives and mining. That didn't stop the Palace's being short two footmen for a while. They both went to jail.

At one of the staff meetings, the question of the freezing temperature of the Nissen-type huts at Balmoral came up. The brigadier had heaters installed—something of a triumph. Royals don't mind what they spend at Buckingham Palace as long as it is done discreetly because the Department of the Environment pays. They do mind what they spend at Balmoral, because the money for that, it being a private house, has to come from the Queen's own purse.

But there are many staff "perks." We'd get apples and turkeys from Sandringham at discount prices, and at Christmas every member of the staff was given a Christmas pudding and crackers. The tenants of the Duchy of Cornwall, the estate that gives Prince Charles his income, all receive hampers from him at Christmas. However, some people are never satisfied. In 1982 some tenants complained that the hampers contained French cheeses. Why wasn't the Prince buying British? they wanted to know. But I did notice that they didn't quibble about the port from Portugal that is always included.

If the Royals get the idea that someone in staff is planning a long career with them, then each Christmas that servant would be given a cup and saucer of fine bone china. Then at his or her own request, via the housekeeper, the following year another, or a matching plate. This way the housemaids and other staff build up a constantly growing china collection that is a shrine to their Royal employers.

Part of my job as Prince Charles's valet was to handle arrangements for the presents for his godchildren on birthdays and at Christmas. It was not an arduous task, as the Royals follow the same procedure for family as for staff. For example, Marina Ogilvy, Princess Alexandra's daughter and one of the Prince's godchildren, gets china. By the time she is twenty-one she will be the possessor of a pleasant dinner service from Thomas Goode, who are the china suppliers to Royalty. Nothing spectacular, mind you. Something good, but not ridiculously expensive. The set was bought complete when she was born and is kept stored at the Palace. Pieces of the service are taken out twice a year and given to her. This method of gift-buying is considered a hedge against inflation.

The godsons get port, a bottle or two every birthday and Christmas. That I would order up from the Prince's own stock in the cellars.

Probably everyone's favorite perk in the Palace is the staff canteen, where drinks are sold at cost price. It is run by a one-armed man—no bandit!—called Len Cluff, who can open a bottle of Scotch faster than anyone with two arms. His entire role in life is looking after the canteen. It's a large room on the first floor—no seats, and rather like a dive bar. It is also the only place in London where you can get a drink at ten o'clock in the morning. The senior staff were always about in the canteen, an unofficial place for meetings. If you wanted any of the various yeomen, that's where they were to be found. Having one.

But not all the drinking at the Palace was done by the staff in their canteen. Members of the high-level Household do just as well. They drink in the Equerries' Room—another touch of privilege: the drinks are free.

This is generous of the Royals, as the Queen has to pay the same enormous duty on alcohol that everyone else in Britain pays. She and her family are basically nondrinkers. Her usual tipple is Malvern Water. Prince Philip might just have a beer; Princess Anne drinks gallons of Coca-Cola; and Prince Charles and Princess Diana live on lemon refreshers, a homemade lemonade drink.

The prices at the canteen are so low, by British standards, that eventually the Master had to make a rule that relatives and friends were not allowed in. Running the Palace canteen was becoming too expensive. The Royal Yacht canteen is an extension of the same system, but not even duty is paid on the alcohol once the *Britannia* is at sea. Britain has a three-mile limit—alcohol can be bought without paying duty once you are three miles off the coast. As the Queen must never be seen to be breaking the law, this means that the Royal Yacht canteen has to charge normal prices while she is berthed at Cowes on the Isle of Wight for Cowes Regatta Week (a racing occasion much enjoyed by Prince Philip). But once the *Britannia* is three miles out—well, it's Mardi Gras!

The crew of the Royal Yacht, though paid by the navy, consider themselves Royal staff too. Indeed, they are frequently borrowed when the Queen needs more help for special occasions. Royal Ascot Week is one of the times when some of the crew come ashore to help out at Windsor for the Queen's house party during the week of racing.

It is a yearly reunion of old mates, when the Palace and the Yacht staffs get together to exchange news. Not unnaturally, they congregate in the canteen at Windsor, which is run on exactly the same lines as the one at Buckingham Palace.

Lunch at Windsor during Royal Ascot Week is always early, so that the Royal Family can get themselves into the carriages to be driven to the course, and then along it, for the crowds to see them.

Before lunch, drinks are served to the Royals and their guests in the Green Drawing Room. I remember one year, when I was acting as page because Prince Charles was in the navy, I was in attendance at the pre-lunch gathering. The drinks are served on vast silver trays, held by a footman. There is a positive arrangement: whisky and gin-and-tonic to the back of the tray, the glasses ranging down in size so that the sherry is at the front.

A footman had been in the canteen all morning. He was standing to attention, hanging on to his tray like grim death, as if it might just keep him upright. In the air around him there was a distinct smell of beer, which is *not* served in the Green Drawing Room at Windsor. Suddenly there was an almighty crash. He had dropped the lot. Silver, crystal, and spilt drinks were all over the patterned carpet.

Someone hustled him away. Someone else quickly cleared up the mess. The Queen never so much as raised an eyebrow. She simply made signals that perhaps it was time to go in to lunch.

Though, in moments of disaster, she acts as if nothing has happened, the Queen applies chapter and verse afterwards. The footman was lucky. He was not sacked, although he had already been given three warnings. It is difficult to sack anyone in Britain these days; being the Queen makes for no exception.

But justice can be swift when the Sovereign is the plaintiff. Kent, a county near London, has a technical college of catering called Thanet, which has become the recruiting ground for Royal footmen. Not so long ago two of their number were on their way home to Kent for the weekend, having visited the canteen before leaving the Palace. They were chattering away most indiscreetly about their work—apparently not mincing words about their Royal employers.

Unfortunately for them, they were in Monarchist territory. An appalled lady passenger on the same train heard every word of their conversation. She saw fit to write to the Palace, saying that, if this was the standard of Royal staff, she felt very sorry for the Queen! The culprits were quickly identified, and given twenty-four hours to get themselves back to Thanet. Permanently.

Much more popular is the young footman Paul Wybrew, who came to the Queen's rescue the morning she woke to find an intruder sitting on her bed. Paul is a pleasant, unassuming lad. Now one of his duties is to look after the Queen's twelve corgis. She always takes him with her when she goes to visit the kennels at Windsor.

Footmen drop clangers; so do other people. At Windsor the Queen once decided that she would move a valuable tapestry from the State apartments into the private apartments. The Superintendent of the Castle was given instructions to get the work done. With some difficulty he and a couple of workmen got the tapestry off the wall, lugged it down to the private apartments and into the room where they had been told to hang it, over an enormous sideboard.

Unfortunately, it was too long. It dropped below the top of the piece of furniture. Someone just cut off the bottom end of the tapestry so that it rested neatly on top of the sideboard. The Queen was furious. The damage was done —at great cost. But there wasn't a lot she could do about it, since it was she who had given the order for the tapestry to be rehung. She is so busy that if someone makes a suggestion about where to move something, she rarely has time to check it out for herself. Once she has agreed to a particular course of action, it is always carried out, regardless.

Because I had been Nursery Footman and, therefore, part of Prince Andrew's childhood, he was always friendly towards me. At Balmoral, in the silver pantry, there is a clean, long, scrubbed table that was used by the staff for table tennis in the evenings. We'd be playing, deep in the servants' quarters, when a head would pop round the door. Prince Andrew's.

"Can I have a game?" he'd ask.

It was part of the same syndrome, I'm sure, that sent Lady Diana scuttling to the kitchens for company when she stayed at Buckingham Palace before the wedding. The kitchens in any great or small house are warm, welcoming places, and Buckingham Palace is no exception.

When the Princes Andrew and Edward were little, they were always going down to see what was cooking. It was there that they'd pick up the odd naughty word. With a team of three chefs, sous-chefs, kitchen maids and porters cooking for nearly three hundred people, if someone dropped a pan or burnt himself, he wasn't going to say "Oh dear!" or even "Damn!"

It is unusual for the Royals to go near the kitchens once they are grown up. I know for a fact that Prince Charles has forgotten the way. After the pre-wedding party for four hundred guests he said to me, "I must go down and thank the chef."

"I'll let him know you are coming, sir," I said, knowing that Peter Page, the Head Chef, would be delighted. He had produced the most superb buffet.

"Where, exactly, are the kitchens?" the Prince asked, adding, "I haven't been there for thirteen years."

I said I would take him, and then rang Peter Page.

"What do you want?" Page asked me suspiciously, expecting a moan or more work.

"Relax," I said. "The Prince wants to come down and thank you. White hat on, and no drinks until he's been."

"Okay," he said, "thanks for letting me know."

I could imagine the resulting scene—everyone looking around for clean white chefs' hats and aprons; cigarettes hidden; kitchen maids polishing everything in sight. But the Prince ran out of time with so much party going on, and we never did get to the kitchen.

Occasionally the kitchen will receive a surprise visit, usually from the Duke of Edinburgh, who will have come to complain. I remember one time when the Queen went to look at the kitchens at Windsor. Michael Sealey, who had been working for her for close to twenty years, was duty chef. She caught him and his staff just clearing up after lunch.

Graciously, she thanked him for a delicious meal, and then made her stately way back to her part of the Castle. En route, she passed the Yeoman of the Glass and China.

She asked, "What's the name of that chef who's on duty today?"

"Michael Sealey, Your Majesty," he said, scarcely able to conceal his glee at the question. The minute the Queen was out of sight, he shot back downstairs to the kitchen.

"Oh, it *was* you, Michael," he said silkily. "The Queen couldn't remember you at all."

Michael was furious, and went around banging the pots and muttering about "seventeen years!" That afternoon, he poured out his anger to me in the large kitchen. Not long afterwards, a job with the Queen Mother came up at Clarence House. He applied, and got it.

It is understandable that those who work for the Queen are happiest when she seems to know and appreciate them. For many years her chauffeur was a man called Harry Purvey. Now, chauffeurs are inclined to be a dull bunch, perhaps because they are attached to the Royal Mews and all play second fiddle to the horses. The Queen and Sir John Miller, the Crown Equerry, both adore the stables occupants and are not too interested in whatever is in the garages. The superb Rolls-Royce with the movable solid silver mascot of Saint George and the Dragon on the bonnet, which is used on state occasions, is vastly inferior in their eyes to anything pulled by horses.

Purvey has retired to a grace-and-favor cottage at Sandringham now, with a farewell present of a corgi from the Queen, but in his day he always drove her to Windsor on Friday afternoons. The Queen was always accompanied by her detective, Commander Michael Trestrail (who has also left her service).

Once at Windsor, Purvey would settle himself down with a cup of tea in the staff room and begin. "The Queen told me . . . " he'd say. "As Her Majesty said to me . . . " Trestrail, who knew that the Queen had said precious little, and that Purvey was just repeating the normal little courtesies, would lift his eyes to heaven and sit there in silence.

On Purvey's retirement we were all convinced that he chose Sandringham, rather than other retirement homes on the various estates, so that he could still catch an occasional glance of the Queen for six weeks of the year. He also has a marvelous little blue MG car that he looks after for Prince Charles. He is allowed to use it himself for a rental of £100 a year, which he pays to the Prince of Wales's office. The car was offered to me, but, maddeningly, I couldn't drive at the time. I would have loved to have it.

Normally, old Royal cars go into a car museum at Sandringham—with entrance fees given to charity after costs have been deducted—and believe me, they keep them long enough to become museum pieces. The Duke of Edinburgh's ancient Lagonda is there, and the Prince's present Aston Martin, now fifteen years old, will undoubtedly land up there, too.

The Royal Family do acknowledge an obligation to house their long-service staff when, like Purvey, they retire. So many are getting old now, however, that finding room for them all is becoming a problem. There are now more staff on pension than there have ever been. On retirement, they can choose where they would like to live, London, Sandringham, or Balmoral, where the grounds are littered with cottages. Or there is Windsor, where the Duke of Edinburgh built a row of quite hideous houses known to us all as "the council estate." They are tucked from public view in Old Windsor. Being new, they are convenient to run. But most people still opt for windy Sandringham because, before the Royal Family became so large, Christmas was always celebrated at Sandringham; Windsor didn't feature at all. Many of the staff married Norfolk girls, the county where Sandringham is situated, and old staff are nostalgic about the place.

In the main the staff are well-housed at all times. Mrs. Fenwick, who is in charge of breeding the corgis and who looks after the Queen's dogs when she is on tour, lives in a pretty little Gothic house in Windsor Great Park. Her husband, head gamekeeper for the Windsor estate, has a house full of dogs. He is always sweeping them off the furniture in a surreptitious way, so as not to upset either his wife or the Queen.

The Royal Mews at Buckingham Palace is like a little village. With the exception of the Crown Equerry, Sir John Miller, not many of the people who work and live there come to the Palace for meals. They have their own apartments or small houses. The coachmen and the postilions live in the Mews. These men are mostly ex-army, either from the Brigade of Guards or one of the cavalry regiments. The Mews also houses all the married men serving in the Palace.

A couple of grand houses back onto the Mews at the corner of Grosvenor Gardens. One used to belong to the King's valet, Jerome, now long retired. If I had stayed and married, it is entirely likely that the beautiful eighteenth-century house would have been mine. At the moment it is occupied by James McDonald, the valet who found King George VI dead in his bed at Sandringham. James then became Prince Philip's valet, and has now retired.

Next door is the home of the Superintendent of the Royal Mews, Major Phelps. Sir John Miller, who is in overall charge, lives in the grandest house of all—big, detached, and elegant. His job as Crown Equerry is one of the most important at the Palace. But the Royal lifestyle needs everyone, down to the man who spends his life mowing the lawns, the man at Windsor who feeds the budgerigars and doves, and the coal porters.

The coal porters haven't seen coal for years, as every one of the Royal homes is now centrally heated with oil. Jobs change with the times, but the titles remain the same. The coal porters now cart luggage, though the Palace, holding to tradition, still has them on the books as coal porters.

I suppose the Palace is no different from anywhere else, in that those who live and work there hate change. The young footman who took over from me as Prince Charles's valet had his problems with the "Old Guard" at the Palace.

Conflicts happen all the time. Oldtime staff have long memories; they still talk about the early days after the Queen's Coronation in 1953, when she moved into Buckingham Palace with her own entourage.

This, too, was following tradition. When the Monarch dies, all the staff have to retire on six months' notice. If the new Monarch does not wish to reemploy them, they are pensioned off.

When the Queen and Prince Philip came to Buckingham Palace with their two small children Prince Charles and Princess Anne, they kept most of the King's employees. But the old staff bitterly resented the new arrivals from Clarence House. Bennett and another page, Bill Holloway, had to fight their way through this barrier of loyalty.

No doubt—hopefully, in the *far* distant future—when Prince Charles becomes King, the same thing will happen all over again.

Chapter Two

AND ALL THE QUEEN'S WOMEN

IT IS PROBABLY BEGINNING TO SOUND AS IF THE PALACE employs only men. In fact, women are employed, but not many, and most serve as housemaids.

In Royal service, housemaids rank below footmen, though, like footmen, they generally arrive very young, either to stay on until they retire or capture a husband en route.

If they marry, they have to leave; the Palace does not employ married women. There were three sisters who came into service while I was there—the Hamilton girls, from a Scottish family living near Balmoral. One married Cyril Dickman, the Palace Steward; the second married Tony Jarred, who is the Deputy Page of the Chambers; and the third became the wife of Johnny Wood, one of the best chefs in the Palace and a very good sportsman. All three had to leave. The only husband and wife act allowed in the Palace is the Queen and Prince Philip.

Housemaids are neither seen nor heard by the Royals. They do their work in either the early mornings or early evenings, just before dinner, while the family and guests are either changing or resting. Any suggestion of anyone appearing—and they melt into the woodwork. Indeed, they acquire a great facility for disappearing.

This is not always easy. Early one evening at Barnwell Manor, in the days of the crusty late Duke of Gloucester, a housemaid was cleaning the stairs outside his dressing room. Normally you can set your watch by the Royals (with the exception of the Queen Mother), but suddenly the Duke appeared, about ten minutes earlier than usual. The maid, Annie, heard the door opening and fled, but the only place she could find to hide was in the closet on the stairs. Quickly she slipped inside and pulled shut the door behind her.

As the Duke came down the stairs, he opened the closet door. "Goodnight, Annie," he said. And closed it on her again.

The same thing once happened with Queen Mary, but she let the maid out. "Don't hide, my dear," she said. "I like to see people around the place."

The twenty-four or so housemaids who are employed by the Queen are kept segregated. They live in the righthand corner of the Palace, and the footmen are at the lefthand corner, though both are on the third floor.

When the housemaids travel to other houses, they are all popped into one bus. They used to be given travel warrants for the Green Line Bus for travel out of London, but the Palace Steward decided it would be cheaper to hire a bus. So now they all move about like convent schoolgirls, with no chance of their being molested, as the Palace Steward piously put it.

One other archaic Palace rule is that footmen are never allowed into ladies' bedrooms, with the result that breakfast trays mostly have to be served by housemaids. When we had a full house at Balmoral or Sandringham, every old, battered tray that could be found was pressed into service and then laden down with wonderful breakfast silver and china. More often than not, they would end up far too heavy for the girls to carry. Breakfast, then, is perforce carried in by the men, with the housemaid hovering in the doorway to make sure nothing untoward takes place.

"As if anyone would want to leap into bed with those old dowagers anyway" is a frequent grumble heard from both the footmen and the maids, who aren't too keen on serving breakfast in any case.

There are certain times when the "not seen/not heard" rules for housemaids are relaxed. On great State occasions they are allowed to watch the pageant and see the Queen go by. This is not permitted for male staff. But the housemaids, in their black dresses, the older ones wearing their long-service medals, may line the corridors as the Queen and her guest of honor go into the state banquets.

The Household grumble because, if a housemaid is needed about fifteen minutes before dinner, one can never be found. The women have all rushed off to watch the parade.

Of course, sometimes they do get blasé about the opportunity, but not during the visit of President Reagan. They were in every corridor at Windsor on the route to the State dining room, pressed back against the walls, quiet as mice, to watch the President and his lady go by with the Queen and Prince Philip. The Pope, I recall, had a similar turnout.

There are few women at the Palace with good jobs. And since Prince Charles's black female secretary left, I'm afraid you never see a black face. A lot that happens in the modern world passes the Royals by.

There is always a Chief Lady Clerk in charge of all the women secretaries. The last Chief Lady Clerk, Miss Jean Taylor, who left recently, was made a Dame. She came to the Palace after having been a Wren (Women's Royal Naval Service) officer. Mrs. DeTre White, the Head Housekeeper, is also ex-WRNS. Though there is a resident housekeeper in all Royal homes, Mrs. DeTre White is the queen bee, in charge of all. A formidable lady who makes unexpected visits to ensure that everything is in order, she is something of a *grande dame,* and not one you'll find with a dust mop in her hand. Nor has she probably ever held one, since she did not work her way up through the ranks of the housemaids.

One of the privileges of being the housekeeper is to be called "Mrs." without ever having had a husband. This is a peculiar British custom that dates back to before Georgian days.

As Head Housekeeper, Mrs. DeTre White oversees the entire staff of women. She has easy access to the Queen, mainly because her job includes seeing to the comfort and the housing of the Queen's guests. She knows which of the hundreds of rooms in the various houses have been redecorated. The Queen relies on her to make suggestions as to which rooms would be most suitable for the many dignitaries and V.I.P. visitors who must be entertained.

Mrs. DeTre White is also allowed to leave the Palace by the front gates—no mean privilege. There is an absolute pecking order about who gets to leave through the front of the Palace instead of skulking out the side door. Incidentally, the side door used to be called the Tradesmen's Entrance, but at the time of the recent Royal marriage, this was changed. Wedding presents for the Prince and Princess were being delivered there, and their donors might have felt insulted by the "tradesmen" label.

Obviously, members of the Household and the gentlemen and ladies-in-waiting are front-gate people. So are senior Officials and some senior Staff, including valets and dressers. In the late King's days, the front-gate people were not allowed to be seen leaving the Palace—even by the side door—without wearing a suit, tie, and hat. None of your jeans and jerseys, like today.

A woman, "Bobo" McDonald, holds what is probably the best job in the Palace: dresser, maid, and confidante to the Queen. Margaret McDonald is definitely high in the staff hierarchy. Nearing eighty now, she has always been a front-gate person, but these days she is driven through. I doubt if she has gone anywhere without a chauffeur for years.

Bobo was nanny to the Queen when she was the small Princess Elizabeth of York, and she is absolutely devoted to her mistress. They even look alike, though, of course, Bobo —or Miss McDonald, as practically all the staff call her—is much older. They have the same hairdo, which is not surprising, since after Charles Martin, the Queen's hairdresser, has finished the Royal head, he moves down the corridor and attends to Bobo's. Their clothes are similar for the same reason. Bobo shops most of the time for the Queen and arranges for designer collections to be presented at the Palace. More often than not, the couturiers who create for Her Majesty will also run up a little something for Bobo. She is an elegant and charming old lady.

She is also a character. Most of the Household and Staff are terrified of her, being well aware of her influence with and closeness to the Queen. When traveling, the first person to be served her meals after the Queen is Bobo. And the Queen's first concern is always that the old lady is being properly looked after. On a plane once, I remember one of the private secretaries saying, "Thank God, we can relax. Bobo's had her breakfast!"

She was always very kind and friendly to me. Once we shared a plane journey during which she had me riveted with tales of her younger days. Though Bobo has devoted her life to Royalty, it seems she didn't miss out on men friends. Most people are not quite sure how to deal with her, because of her proximity to the Queen, with whom she even shared the same bedroom when the Queen was a little girl. She has been with her mistress for over fifty years, having come into Royal service at the age of fifteen, as a nursery maid. Eventually she was picked by the Queen Mother to be nanny to the small Princess Elizabeth and Princess Margaret Rose. Since then, wherever the Queen has gone, Bobo has gone too.

There was a rumor in the Palace in the early days of my service that the Queen Mother and Bobo did not get on well because the Queen Mother was resentful of Bobo's influence on her daughter. It is true that the Queen Mother and Miss McDonald have little to say to each other. But I once saw them meet by chance in the Palace corridors: they exchanged warm pecks on the cheek. And the Queen Mother always buys Bobo an extra-special present at Christmas.

Bobo was left behind only once when the Queen went on one of her tours. In 1974, the Queen was going to Australia, and Bobo had fallen and broken a bone. It was decided she had better stay in England, as the journey was grueling, and would certainly be too much for her. She was highly indignant.

"I shall manage very well," she said in the Scottish burr that she has never lost.

Nevertheless, she was left behind, full of gloom at the prospect of nothing to do for six weeks, with her beloved mistress on the other side of the world.

During the trip there was a Government crisis. Edward Heath, Prime Minister at the time, was involved in a political collision with the miners. He lost, and his defeat forced an election. The Queen, as head of state, had to return from Australia immediately.

Bobo was delighted. "There you are," she said to the chef, "the first time the Queen's ever had to go away without me, and now she's back. I knew it would all go wrong if I wasn't there."

She is so dismayed if she is left behind that the next time

she broke a bone—she is at an age when she does fall a lot
—the Queen decided to take her on a Royal Yacht cruise,
regardless. She had to be lowered on and off, which caused
a lot of grumbling among the crew, but she herself was game
for anything, as long as she wasn't away from the Queen.
She may be solicitous of her mistress, but the Queen is
equally solicitous of her.

To commemorate Bobo's fifty years of Royal service, the
Queen secretly commissioned a very special present for her.
It was a brooch, made in the shape of a flower with twenty-
five stamens which had tiny diamonds on the tips of twenty-
five simple stems of gold. This represented the fifty years of
the Crown (the diamonds) and Bobo (the gold) together.
Garrard & Company, the Crown jewelers, designed and specially made it.

For once Bobo was lost for words. She was absolutely
delighted by her Royal mistress's gesture.

But things don't always go smoothly with Bobo. I can
remember one occasion at Balmoral, when Bobo was going
back to London ahead of the main party. Lord Snowdon,
Princess Margaret's husband at the time, was staying at the
castle. He, too, was returning to London for his work. The
Queen, in the interests of economy, asked if he would mind
traveling in the car with Bobo for the sixty-mile drive to
Aberdeen Station. And would he look after her? Lord Snowdon, a man of great charm, said he would not mind in the
least.

Prince Charles and I returned from a fishing afternoon
to find him waiting for Bobo in the large open hallway of
Balmoral Castle. I was putting the Prince's rods away in
the corner where they are always left, while he chatted to
his mother and Lord Snowdon. At that moment, Bobo
appeared, escorted by her two assistant dressers, who
had deserted their ironing and mending to be of more immediate help to their mistress. I fear it was more than obvious that Bobo had had one or two more sherries than

were good for her at lunchtime. She was having problems navigating.

Lord Snowdon's face was a picture.

I caught the Prince's eye, and we both dissolved into hysterical giggles. The Queen gave us a reproving look, but she had to hurry away into one of the rooms off the hall to hide her own laughter. I'm afraid we left Lord Snowdon to cope, all of us going off in different directions.

Upstairs in his room the Prince, still laughing, said, "Did you see her, Stephen?" Then he paused and thought for a moment before adding, "I suppose one day you'll end up like that."

"Thank you very much, sir," I said smartly, not pleased.

Thinking about the remark now, it seems obvious that he thought I would remain his valet in the same way that Bobo had remained his mother's dresser.

Bobo disapproves of Prince Philip, and he in turn keeps her firmly in her place. As far as he's concerned, she's someone fit to open the curtains in the mornings and let the dogs in—duties she has performed for the Queen's entire adult life.

Nor could Princess Margaret's dresser and nanny stand Lord Snowdon. It was mutual there too. Princess Alexandra's dresser has never said a word to the Princess's husband, Angus Ogilvy—not so far as anyone has noticed, anyway.

Those staff with their "own" Royals guard them jealously and really can't stand anyone else on their patch. To the elderly women who have spent their lives caring for Princesses and Queens, husbands are an intrusion. The Royal nannies, for example, have always been a law unto themselves. Mabel Anderson, who brought up all the Queen's children, had her own little apartment, her own footman, and was loved and highly regarded by the Royal Family.

I suspect it is a disappointment to both the Queen and Prince Charles, who adored Mabel, that she is not in charge of Prince William. When he was born, she had already moved on from the Royal Family. It was perhaps just as well, since Princess Diana wanted a younger, more modern nanny to bring up her son. Since Nanny Anderson is happy with another family now and keeps in constant touch with Prince Charles, all has worked out well.

Nannies are very much a part of Royal life, and they have an enormous effect on the children. People sometimes say that the Queen has the outlook and views of a sensible Scottish railwayman's daughter. And if she has, it is hardly surprising, since the main influence in her life has always been Bobo McDonald, who is just that.

And there is no doubt that Mabel Anderson, a Scottish policeman's daughter, had a great deal to do with forming the kind, thoughtful character of Prince Charles. She wasn't so successful with Prince Andrew, but then, he was always a little demon.

When Mabel was on holiday in those days, a Nanny Bunn used to come in and take over the care of Prince Andrew and Prince Edward. She was a plump, jolly lady, very old-fashioned; she could have been instantly cast for the Nurse in *Romeo and Juliet*.

The curious thing was that Prince Philip, who never spoke to Nanny Anderson if he could possibly avoid it, was fond of Nanny Bunn. He would suggest to her that she bring the children down to have lunch with him if he was eating alone. I could never understand it. The only explanation that ever came to mind—other than that he just enjoyed her company—was that perhaps she reminded him of his own nanny, from long ago.

It could have been so, because many Royals are most at ease with those who serve them. The servants are the source of their comfort, and, for the children, sometimes the source of genuine warmth and affection. This is not to say that the Royals don't love their children. Of course they do; a great deal. But they themselves were brought up in a system in which they were cared for by others, their parents having what they would think of as better things to do than change nappies.

And the system continues.

Among the characters who work for the Queen, one must not forget "the Edinburgh women." Come the ten weeks' holiday at Balmoral, extra staff members are needed for the house parties and to run the huge houses. The Edinburgh women come year after year, a busload of them, mostly widows—fat, jolly ladies for whom the ten weeks of working for Royalty is the treat of the year. Over the years many of them have died, but their daughters take their places, and then, eventually, their grandchildren.

They are very much part of the Royal scene. We all had sing-songs with them in the canteen. They are invited to the Ghillies' Ball, the highlight of the holiday, where they all arrive in a wash of polyester, with their hair newly done. Prince Charles and Prince Philip make a point of dancing with as many of them as possible. Both men enjoy it, even if it is, as Prince Charles once remarked, rather ruefully, "like dancing with a marquee!"

The Edinburgh women are housed in Balmoral itself, two to a room. They are not well paid, but the pay helps their pensions, and they have a lot of fun. If they didn't, they wouldn't return year after year. And, full of life and down to earth as they are, they made the place a lot more fun for us.

Of course, there are many more people involved in the oiling of the Royal wheels than I have mentioned—gardeners, grooms, maintenance engineers, electricians. It is rather a mixture of running a vastly rich home and an enormously rich business.

All the Queen's men and women enjoy the cachet of working for her. But how does she feel about them?

The Royals have mixed feelings about their helpers. In many cases, there is a genuine affection, concern, and interest. But at the end of the day most of the Royals wish the staff were out of sight and a million miles away. They think of us as a necessary evil.

But the truth of the matter is that, without their servants, most Royals would be very lonely.

Chapter Three

THE QUEEN, HER HOME, HER HISTORY

I ENJOYED LIVING AT BUCKINGHAM PALACE FOR THE TWELVE years that I was Prince Charles's valet. I had my own rooms at the back, overlooking forty acres of superb garden; constant service; a housemaid to clean; footmen to run errands, if I needed a bottle of vodka from the canteen (at cost price); meals cooked; and a cheerful club in the shape of the bar at the canteen.

And, of course, it was a very good address.

On the other hand, the Royal Family themselves loathe living at BP (as we call the Palace). The Queen—and Prince Philip, if he is in England, which isn't often—are stuck with it for five days a week. On Friday afternoon at 2:30 they are off like a shot to Windsor Castle, which they consider their real home. The rest of the Royals avoid staying at the Palace as much as they possibly can—with the exception, that is, of

Prince Andrew. When they are forced to spend a night there, anyone would think they were being housed in a stable, what with the fuss they make.

Prince Charles used to say, "I hate being in London. It's the weekend, and we're stuck. I can't bear it."

In fact, the Queen and Prince Philip really only *have* to stay at the Palace for one Saturday night a year. This is early in November, when they go to the Albert Hall for the Festival of Remembrance for two world wars. On Sunday morning they leave from the Palace for the Remembrance Day service at the Cenotaph in Whitehall. They also have to stay one Friday night before the Trooping of the Color ceremony— the second weekend in June—but they're off to Windsor immediately after that's over.

Though the Palace is large and gloomy, it is still luxurious by anyone's standards, as long as one is on the right side of the green baize door that divides Royals from staff. But even so, the family hate spending any of their free time in London. Times change; in the old days, Queen Mary and King George V, the Queen's grandmother and grandfather, never left the city on weekends. King George loved Sandringham, and Queen Mary was fond of badminton in Gloucestershire, which is the home of her niece, the Duchess of Beaufort. But in both cases, the country was reserved only for holidays.

The Queen's parents, George VI and the present Queen Mother, reigned throughout the Second World War, and felt it would be unpatriotic to flee too far from London during weekends. They did manage brief visits to Royal Lodge. This house in Windsor Great Park was their home before George became King.

If possible, the Queen avoids overnight entertaining at the Palace. Even if the Queen's and Prince Philip's closest friends come to London, they will not be offered a bed for the night, but would be expected to make their own arrangements. Only heads of state get to stay at the Palace—and one of the Queen Mother's godchildren, Denis Dawnay. More on him later.

The Royals have good reason for not using the Palace as a hotel. Curiously, for such an enormous building, there are very few guest bedrooms. Out of six hundred rooms, there are just about a dozen suites. It is, as I have already said, more an office than a home.

When the Royal Standard comes down on a Friday afternoon, the Queen's thirteen-year-old Rover draws away from the Privy Purse Gate to take her to Windsor for the weekend. The Queen's flag orderly, up on the roof, stands by the flagpole waiting to see the Rover move off. He then lowers her standard, a signal to all in the Palace that the weekend has begun. The old Rover is always used for the journey, as it is less recognizable in the Friday-night traffic than her official Rolls-Royces—the only six cars in Britain without license plates.

Without the Queen, the vast, musty building dies. With its endless corridors and underground passages, it becomes almost creepy. The housemaids put away their dusters and brooms, the footmen go off for the weekend, the lights go out. Only a skeleton staff of maintenance and security men is left. When Her Majesty returns on Monday, the place springs back to life again. It is as if the building itself needs her presence.

On her departure from Windsor, the staff there watch for the car to drive off, and then lower the flag over the castle. The routine is the same: the minute she leaves, one of her two pages—the one who has been on duty for the weekend —will telephone his opposite number in London.

"The Queen has left," he says.

Approximately forty minutes later the Queen's car will sweep through the gates at Buckingham Palace. As if by magic, her page and her footman will arrive at the garden entrance. Actually, the magic consists of the duty policeman on the gate pressing a warning button the moment the car is in sight.

The flag orderly is in his place on the roof, rain or shine, also keeping an eagle eye out for the car. As it drives through the gate, up goes her standard. The flag orderly is borrowed from the army, and when not on the roof, he works as an orderly in the Master of the Household's office.

The Queen insists on having her standard flying if the Court is in residence. She was furious one time when she went out for the day at Balmoral, and the caretaker, who is in charge of the flag there, took it down. The flag is flown wherever the Queen is actually staying, never when she has left for somewhere else.

There is no question that the Queen is the heart and the hub of Royalty. I realized this clearly when Prince Charles was in the navy, and to fill in my time I was working as a page at the Palace. I saw then how everything revolves around her. Until Prince Charles's wedding to Lady Diana Spencer, the Queen was undoubtedly the most popular woman in Britain. Princess Diana has supplanted her in this position, but the Queen is not upset in the least. Others of the Royal ladies might be showing a touch of jealousy. But the Queen has been heard to say now that the Princess has settled down, she has given Royalty a fresh, youthful image that can only be for the good.

If the Crown is to survive—and the burden of ensuring that has rested on the Queen's shoulders for over thirty years now—the new generations of Royalty must capture the affections of the British public in the same way that she herself did as the young Princess Elizabeth.

In 1977, when the Queen held her Silver Jubilee celebrations, even she was astonished by the love and affection shown to her by people the length and breadth of Britain. She honestly had not expected such a response.

I remember the morning of the Jubilee Thanksgiving Service, when the Queen was going to ride in the State Coach to St. Paul's Cathedral. As Prince Charles was getting ready to accompany her, he looked out of his bedroom window, facing onto the Mall, and exclaimed, "Stephen! Look at the people! Will we ever get through? I can't believe it."

Well, they got through, and it was a day to remember. The Queen herself was almost bewildered when she left the Grand Entrance to the Palace. Her Staff—housemaids, footmen, pages, chef—were waiting to see her leave. They actually clapped and cheered as she appeared, breaking all the rules. Staff were both seen and heard in the Palace on that occasion.

This disregard for the rules delighted the Queen that day. She left the Palace smiling and happy. She relaxed, though it was in her usual reserved way. I used to marvel at how she never stopped being "Her Majesty." Until I realized that it is built in.

How could it not be? She is the Queen of ten nations. Her full rank and title is: "Elizabeth the Second, by the Grace of God, of the United Kingdom of Great Britain, Northern Ireland and her other realms and territories, Queen, Head of the Commonwealth, Defender of the Faith." She was the first Sovereign to be proclaimed Head of the Commonwealth.

All of which adds up to more than one billion subjects.

It's hardly surprising she can get a bit grand on occasions!

At the Palace there are still some Royal employees who go back a long, long way. They know that the sense of being Royal was instilled in the Queen by her mother when she was still a little girl. It was, of course, an accident of fate that she and her mother ever became Queens. If Edward VIII had not fallen in love with Wallis Simpson, a twice-divorced American woman who was totally unacceptable to the British at that time, history would have been changed. The Queen would have remained Princess Elizabeth of York. Apart from undertaking her share of Royal duties, she would have lived a happy, private life in the country, sur-

THE QUEEN, HER HOME, HER HISTORY

rounded by the dogs and horses she adores. Her children would probably have been closer in age. It was simply not possible for her to continue her family immediately upon becoming Queen, which is why there is such a big age gap between Andrew and Edward.

One can only guess at whether she would have been happier or not.

As it was, King Edward abdicated to marry Mrs. Simpson, the woman he loved. The Duke of York—the Queen's father —a shy man with a stammer, was suddenly elevated to the throne. All this is an oft-told tale, of course, but what many people don't realize is that George VI would never have succeeded in becoming George the Good—as the British called him—without the supporting strength of his seemingly fluffy, friendly, charming wife, born Lady Elizabeth Bowes-Lyon.

She came from aristocratic stock. Her father was the Earl of Strathmore, but she was not Royal, nor had she been brought up to be so. Yet she put the backbone in the new King. According to one retired page, she also taught her elder daughter what being Royal means. She made both her children, Elizabeth and Margaret Rose, curtsy to their father. She reasoned this would help him accept that the Sovereign must of necessity be apart from other men. She also felt that it would make the children sharply aware of the majesty of the Monarchy, if they were made to treat their father first as the King.

When I first entered Royal service, old Palace retainers would tell stories of the little Princess Elizabeth and how well her mother's lessons had been learned. And the lessons of her grandmother Queen Mary.

One day while out with Queen Mary, she was being helped down from a carriage.

"Down you come, young lady," said the footman who was lifting her.

"I am not," said Elizabeth, aged eleven, "a young lady. I am a Princess."

"And," said her grandmother tartly, "one day we hope you will be a lady, too."

The daughter of one of Queen Elizabeth's court dressmakers, now the same age as the Queen, remembers running up to her at a Buckingham Palace children's party.

"I had just been given a small present," she recalls, "and I was thrilled and wanted to show it to the Princess. 'Look, look,' I said.

"The Princess gave me a cold stare. 'Curtsy, girl, curtsy,' she said."

Though that remoteness and demand for respect is still part of the Queen's public character, she is a warm and kind woman in private. She could not have been nicer to me.

I remember once at Sandringham I had been plodding along behind the Prince, out shooting. He had bagged pheasants by what seemed like the score. He had worn me out.

I decided to hang about and wait on one of the country lanes until he returned. Suddenly a Land-Rover appeared, with the Queen at the wheel. She saw me and stopped immediately.

"Are you all right, Stephen?" she asked.

"Just waiting for His Royal Highness, Your Majesty," I said.

"Oh, he'll be ages," she said. "Jump in."

And she drove me back to Sandringham House.

A poll among the staff would put her way out on top as the most respected of all the Royals, closely followed by Prince Charles. Among the true insiders, she is much more loved than the public's new darling, Princess Diana. Alas, the one to get the booby prize would be Princess Margaret, because of the hours she keeps and expects the staff to keep too.

THE QUEEN, HER HOME, HER HISTORY

Make no mistake, though. Nobody takes liberties with the Queen.

And if someone does, she has a look that would freeze the sun. Nobody but her immediate family would dream of calling her by her childhood name, Lillibet. No one except her family ever touches her. Dignitaries have made the mistake of trying to take her arm on public occasions, only to find themselves very positively shaken off. She dislikes even being stared at, but that she has to put up with.

What did puzzle her staff, though, on her Canadian tour in 1982, was the remark allegedly made by her Press Secretary, Michael Shea, to a Canadian woman journalist. She reported him as saying the Queen had her "Miss Piggy" face on. None of us had ever said that. We did say "She's doing her mouth" when she was about to get angry, but "Miss Piggy" was a new one to us. It must have been something either he or the journalist had dreamed up.

A story is told about Queen Victoria, the Queen's great-great-grandmother, which the Queen often repeats, probably because it reflects her own situation. In public, Queen Victoria was never amused. The Queen says that when something hilarious happened, Victoria would simply sit there, straightfaced and grim. But those who knew her could tell she was shrieking with laughter inside, because slow tears would be gently running down her passive face.

Queen Elizabeth told that story when she and her family were the stars of a television film. I was working as a footman at the time, and for a year, wherever the Court went, the cameras went. It was 1967; the BBC had requested to make a film about Royalty, using what were then up-to-date *cinéma vérité* methods of filming, with hand-held cameras and directional microphones. They wanted to eavesdrop on the family's real conversation and behavior at home, work, and play.

There was a lot of muttering among the Palace Establishment that it was not a good idea. But Prince Philip, who has always attempted to drag the Monarchy—screaming!—into the twentieth century, argued for the project, so long as there were safeguards.

The "Old Guard" did have a point. Half the appeal of Royalty in those old days was its mystery. But on the condition that the film be okayed by the Queen and the Duke before being shown, the project went ahead. As the "Old Guard" had warned, it did dispel the mystery to some extent. The mystery continues to diminish, but it is being replaced, certainly as far as Princess Diana is concerned, by star quality. And, if anything, this new image of Royalty has enhanced their popularity.

Of course everyone at the Palace was dying to see the film. The sequence in which I took part was filmed in Scotland, at Balmoral. The producer, Richard Cawston, wanted to film the piper walking up and down the grand path outside the Queen's bedroom, as he does every morning at nine. The problem was that the weather was doing what it generally does in Scotland: raining. It was decided to delay the piper until the weather had cleared and so, at five o'clock in the evening, the cameras finally rolled. Someone had to rush around and change the courtyard clock to nine o'clock, then immediately set it right again. The Queen cannot abide clocks to be wrong.

But the piper wasn't pleased, either. His idea of bliss is to play for fifteen minutes in the morning. Then he's off to the canteen, with the rest of the day off, before piping again in the evening after dinner. Round and round the table he usually goes, blowing away. And then he gets Sunday off. So he was quite put out by the upset to his routine.

What came out as a solemn and serious film seemed comical at the time to us. They made great play of the Queen's boxes; the idea was to show how hard she works reading State papers, and how this chore never stops even when she is on holiday. She *does* work hard, but, to be truthful, during the summer months the impressive-looking boxes that arrive by train at Balmoral and come up to the house by post-van are mostly nearly empty.

The scene that had us in the aisles showed a blue State box, seen to be leaving Downing Street (the Prime Minister's office and home) in a car that was then driven through the gates of Buckingham Palace. The box was solemnly taken to the office of Sir Philip Moore, the Queen's Private Secretary, where he opened it with his key. Then—without letting the audience see him do it close up—he put the contents in the red Royal box, which went upstairs to the Queen's sitting room. There she opened that box and took out . . . one measly letter. None of us could understand why the BBC didn't fill the box up with masses of paper if they were intent on making her look busy.

The same boxes made for comedy at Balmoral too. In my humble position as footman, I had to be seen pushing this great big trolley-load of red and blue boxes to the Private Secretary's office. A vast number had arrived, and they looked heavy. In the film I needed help to push them up the hill—in spite of the fact that they were all empty.

Still, the film was a fantastic success and was shown in one hundred and forty countries. In Britain, 23,000,000 people watched it the first night it was shown, including most of the Palace staff. After all, a lot of us were in it. And though we had the odd laugh, most of us agreed it was pretty accurate.

What Richard Cawston did catch was the Queen's sense of humor about the crazier moments of her job. She can be extremely funny about people in a slightly mocking way. She is also a first-class mimic, particularly of politicians. But never to anyone's face. She must never be seen to laugh at anyone, except of course a paid comedian.

But she does laugh in private after meeting some of her subjects. And she does state her opinions of them pretty forcefully. Someone to whom she had been incredibly gracious five minutes before will be described as "bonkers" or "a fool" afterwards. They are two of her favorite words. And she is generally right in her character assessments.

Everyone, too, is "them." "Them" are the staff, the public, the Government. The royal "we" is exactly that, where the Queen is concerned; it refers only to Royalty. People say the Queen has no sense of humor and is too often unsmiling. The truth is that her stern look is frequently no more than an effort to keep a straight face. Most politicians have to reverse out of the room after an audience with her, cautiously backing their way out, praying they don't fall over something. It's hard for her not to let a stray smile escape.

If the Queen didn't get a bit of amusement from what is basically a mind-bogglingly boring job, she'd probably have gone off her head long ago. Imagine having to present nearly a thousand different people with awards, on two separate occasions every year. The Lord Chamberlain's office makes the arrangements for the awards to be given, but they are all personally presented, mostly by the Queen. Other members of the family will lend a hand if the Queen is away. When she goes abroad, two Counselors of State are appointed for the duration of her absence. Princess Anne, Princess Margaret, the Queen Mother, and Prince Charles have all acted as Counselors.

I used to love listening to people after they had received their honors. They would be properly attired in morning dress, with wives or close relations waiting for them. The first question always would be: "What did she say to you?" and the answer generally: "I can't remember."

It fascinated me how people are struck dumb in her presence, which, of course, makes it much harder for her to keep the conversational ball rolling. The person meeting her is generally so busy taking in her appearance and being mesmerized by her quite beautiful eyes that every other thought flies from his or her head. I took my sister to meet her once at a Staff party at Buckingham Palace celebrating the Queen Mother's eightieth birthday. My sister's reaction was exactly the same: she couldn't remember a word the Queen said.

The Steward's Room (Senior Staff) had hosted the party, which we held in our own private room at the Palace. When the Queen heard what we were doing, she said to her page —a member of the same room—that she thought she might come along, too. And she did. The Officials echelon was wild with jealousy.

I often attended the investitures while Prince Charles was in the navy and I was acting as a page. I would stand by the doors in the room where the investitures take place. When they were over and the Queen came into the East Gallery, another page and I would open the doors into the State Dining Room and then close them behind her. As the Queen came through, at about 12:30, you could see her visibly relax, as the corgis came to greet her. The Comptroller of the Lord Chamberlain's office would be there too, basically to say "thank you." She would bestow about one hundred and forty medals, titles, insignia, whatever, and it would have taken her about an hour and ten minutes. The Queen Mother takes much longer with this task, incidentally. She never gets through until at least a quarter to one.

On one particular day, the Queen had just finished what all the Royals considered a very dreary investiture—nothing but professors, teachers, scientists, and doctors being honored. The Royals prefer investitures when there are a few show business people or sportsmen (particularly to do with racing) in the group. But this day had been bereft of anyone of any great interest.

"Phew!" said the Queen to the Comptroller, shaking her head. "Had I tripped in there and had the Lord Chamberlain asked if there was a doctor in the house, I'd have been crushed in the stampede."

Surprisingly, in her long reign the Queen has knighted only one jockey that I can recall—Sir Gordon Richards. One could have expected more, since racing is known as the Sport of Kings in Britain, and is certainly the sport of our Queen.

One of Britain's most famous novelists is an ex-jockey who, before he became a millionaire mystery writer, used to ride the Queen Mother's horses. Just recently the Queen attended a literary reception, and the famous novelist, Dick Francis, was presented to her.

"Ah, yes," she said with a smile. "You were my mother's jockey, weren't you?"

No one who knew her was surprised. She is sent thousands of books a year, but her basic reading is the daily newspapers, particularly the *Daily Telegraph* for the crossword. She also reads *The Sporting Life* and the French racing papers, which are sent up to her room every morning.

Her meeting with Dick Francis must have sparked a memory. In the 1984 New Year Honors List he was given the OBE, the Order of the British Empire.

Racing is very much a part of Royal life. When I first worked at the Palace, Ascot week was marvelous. The Royals and their guests settle down at Windsor Castle for the week, going to the races at Ascot Racecourse every day. They arrive in open carriages driven down the center of the course, while the magnificently dressed racegoers line the rails and hang from their boxes to cheer, champagne glasses in hand.

Until just a few years ago the Castle was always full of European royalty for the week. It was all very formal, with white tie and tails worn by the guests for dinner. The British Royal men wear Windsor dress: a tailcoat jacket with red revers and red bands on the sleeves. This garment was invented by Prince Philip, and is worn with knee breeches and black hose. It is worn only at Windsor. Today, perhaps because of the Queen's obsession with not appearing too extravagant, the style has changed. These days the guests wear black tie and a dinner jacket, and are invited to stay only until Friday evening. As soon as the last race is over, so is their visit, and the Queen is back to the coziness of her own private dining room.

European royalty is no longer seen—not that there is much of it about these days. The guests tend to be landed gentry. Actually, the Queen is not mad about the landed gentry, who do have a tendency to be boring and stuffy.

They are also inclined to be much grander than the Royals. One Duke, who is also one of the richest men in the world, had built a new country seat. Prince Charles dismissed it in one word: "Hideous!" he said. The other Royals agreed; the house is now known to them all as "The Inn on the Park."

The Queen is more content with the wives of her Court Household and her own staff. She is truly happy at dog trials or horse trials with people from the estate, like Meldrum, for example, who looks after the working dogs. To her, this is preferable to the company of those with huge houses and family trees going back to William the Conqueror.

"Much too grand for us," she is liable to remark.

At the end of the day, the Queen is not mad about having too many guests. But she is a superb hostess, and, of course, the standard of living is still far ahead of anyone else's, even if they are reduced to black-tie dinners these days.

The four faithfuls at Ascot are the Queen herself, Princess Margaret, the Queen Mother, and Prince Charles. Prince Philip can't abide horse racing and generally disappears after having driven down the course and done his bit waving to the crowds. He then sits at the back of the Royal Box, where there is a small sitting room, and deals with his letters and paperwork. There is a television set in the room, so he can keep one eye on the cricket. He reappears to escort the Queen to the paddock, and also when the Royal Box serves the most marvelous tea to between thirty and sixty people, before they all go back to Windsor Castle.

It is difficult to imagine just how enormous Windsor Castle is. In my day, when I would accompany Prince Charles there, I was forever finding lost souls wandering around desperately trying to discover the way back to their rooms.

Prince Charles lived in the Queen's Tower then, a vast square of granite, forbidding from the outside, comfortable inside. His rooms were modern by the Castle standard, with bright red curtains and spotlights.

Most of Windsor, though, is steeped in history. Some of the finest paintings in the Royal collection hang on the Castle's silk-covered walls. The State apartments, used by the Queen on formal evenings, have fresco ceilings painted at the time of Charles I. Everything in these State apartments is formal. But the Queen's private sitting room, although overpowered by portraits of her ancestors, has squashy, comfortable sofas, and, in the winter, a blazing open fire. The dogs' water bowls are set under a fine antique table.

Today Prince Charles and Princess Diana live in Lancaster Tower when visiting the Castle. Situated one tower away from the Queen's Tower, it has high ceilings, gilt painted furniture, silk damask curtains, and deep pile carpeting. There is nothing cheap or tawdry at Windsor; there cannot be a grander house. It is the largest occupied castle in the world, and yet it manages to be surprisingly comfortable and welcoming.

The Royal Family use a great deal of its vast accommodations by spreading themselves around. Everyone has a suite. Even the staff never grumble there about their quarters. Nor indeed do the guests who spend either a weekend or Ascot Week there.

Ascot Week is family time. However, when they are all in London, the Queen does not see a great deal of either her mother or her sister. A lot of telephoning goes on, and when the operator puts the Queen through to her mother every morning, he says, "Your Majesty? Her Majesty, Your Majesty." It gives new operators the giggles, but none of them ever knows what is said once the two Majesties are connected. The line is scrambled.

In London the Queen rings her mother, and Princess Margaret rings the Queen, but during holidays they are all family together. Teatimes are meeting times, when they eat huge teas with cucumber sandwiches, cakes, scones—everything one imagines of the English tea. It is hard on the Queen, as she has to watch her weight constantly.

After one of her lengthy tours abroad she comes back home and goes straight onto a grapefruit diet. She is enormously careful not to get overweight, since she has a bit of a sweet tooth. One of her little treats is to dissolve sugar at the bottom of her coffee cup and, when it gets soft and gooey, to eat it with a spoon.

As Prince Philip is away so much, they are often three women together. Alone, that is, except for the hovering staff. And sometimes Captain Dawnay, one of the Queen Mother's godchildren, who is one of the few people allowed to stay at Buckingham Palace. He uses it like a rather posh club. The Queen, who is extremely fond of him, usually dines with him if he is staying there.

Denis Dawnay is a marvel to the staff, because he seems to have *carte blanche* with the Royals. He is the perfect courtier—amusing, witty—and knows how to sing for his supper. His parents died when he was a very young man, and King George V, who was his godfather, took him over. The Royals have been looking after him ever since. He is said to have been dying from a weak heart for some thirty years now, but there is little sign of it.

He and Princess Margaret get on well. She relies on him for tidbits of news from the outside world. They were talking one day about the Palace being overlooked by the Hilton Hotel, and he said, "Oh, ma'am, there's the most wonderful bar up there. Have you been?"

"No," she said, "but we fly past the place in the helicopter and you can just see in. We have to turn right there to get into the Palace grounds."

Dawnay is a wispy, fey man in his late sixties who looks

just like the British actor Charles Hawtrey. When he stays at Balmoral, he is able to escape all sport and exercise because of his ill health. Mr. Dawnay is the lucky one who follows the guns by Land-Rover. He's always at Windsor at Christmas, and he's there again at Easter. And he hates to leave.

"Denis," the Queen will say, "we do have a lot of guests arriving."

"Oh, good," he says blandly, not minding that his room constantly changes.

I remember his leaving Balmoral once and saying plaintively as he went through the door, "I *think* I'll be all right."

"I'm sure you will be, Denis," the Queen, who was seeing him off, said cheerfully.

But they don't seem to mind, and he's always welcome the next time.

Close friends are hard to come by for the Royals. The older servants say that Prince Philip still misses Michael Parker, who was his Equerry for many years at the beginning of the Queen's reign. They were young men in the navy together originally, and always up to harmless mischief. But Michael Parker's marriage had broken up, and at that time, the climate of public opinion would not permit a divorced man so near to the Monarch.

In order to substantiate the Queen's role as "Defender of the Faith," Michael Parker had to go. It is sad for him that the rules have gradually changed. Princess Margaret is the prime example. The break-up of her marriage to Anthony Snowdon caused the Queen much heartache. Princess Diana's parents are divorced, as are the young Duchess of Gloucester's, and Lord Snowdon's were already divorced when he married Princess Margaret. Princess Michael of Kent had been divorced before she married the Prince. The Queen's cousin, Lord Harewood, had a particularly public divorce when he left the pianist Marion Stein to marry a young Australian girl, Bambi Tuckwell. It is becoming increasingly difficult for the Royals to go on shunning divorced people as they did, even in my early days as a footman.

Vestiges of Old Establishment prejudice remain. Divorced people may visit the Queen at Balmoral or elsewhere, but they cannot bring live-in lovers.

Even the films shown at Royal gatherings reflect the "Defender of the Faith" aspect of the Monarchy. Probably the Queen wouldn't mind a naughty film at all, but she feels it would be embarrassing for her guests to see her watching it. So the movies are always for family viewing. There was a time when the Equerry and the Steward had to sit through a film first to make sure that it would meet the Royal standard. The Queen doesn't like to be caught out.

She made one of her rare public judgments when she heard that impresario Lew Grade was to make a film about the life of Christ. It was, she said, an obnoxious thing to do. She does not approve of people making money out of religion.

The high moral standard is supposed to apply to the staff. The only people who are fired at the Palace are those who have done something Her Majesty cannot be seen to be condoning, something criminal or—as she is head of the Church of England—a moral lapse. So people are fired from Royal service only for breaking the law or for sexual offenses. I well remember one unfortunate footman who was sent on his way. He had been assisting Holloway, the Duke of Edinburgh's page.

"Where's Peter today?" the Duke asked Holloway one morning.

"He's been sacked, sir," his page told him.

"What did he do?" grunted the Duke.

"I'm afraid they found him in bed with one of the housemaids, sir."

"And they sacked him!" the Duke said, outraged. "The man should have been given a medal!"

But it distresses the Queen when one of her staff has to

go. She had a footman for some years who was a great success with her, as he showed a considerable interest in racing. Unfortunately, he was guilty of creating a public scandal when he chased a young sailor around the dining room on the Royal Yacht. When the yacht berthed at Aberdeen, on the east coast of Scotland, the sailor complained to the Master of the Household. Immediately upon reaching Balmoral, the footman was fired.

Knowing what was about to happen, the Queen put on her mac, her wellies, and her headscarf, and took the dogs for a long walk. When she came back, he had gone. She had avoided his appealing to her because she is basically kind-hearted and she had personally liked him. But she cannot be seen to accept a controversial situation.

She can never be controversial. She leaves that role to Prince Philip. I remember one dinner when they were talking about something a little on the politically delicate side. The Duke said, "And what do you think, Lillibet?" The Queen immediately looked under the table and said, "Sugar, Sugar, where are you, Sugar?"

Out popped a corgi. The Duke said drily, "That's Lillibet's dog defense mechanism going into action. If she doesn't want to commit herself, she calls the dogs."

The dogs are always there, even at mealtimes, and the Queen will feed them breadsticks under the table. Not that they pester for food. They are far too fat and lazy.

One time a footman left one of the Queen's "Meet the People" lunches, chortling to himself, and looking for an audience to tell what he had just witnessed. Heather, the three-legged corgi, veteran of many battles and now laid to rest at Sandringham, was getting under people's feet. "Heather!" the Queen snapped sternly. "Stop it!"

Heather Harper, an opera-singer guest, nearly jumped out of her skin. Much to Prince Philip's amusement.

In spite of the Queen's and Prince Philip's many differences—he's not keen on corgis or horse racing, is impatient and controversial, and lives an independent life—the marriage is a good one. Except when he has to be up and off early, or comes in very late, they still often share the same king-sized bed. In come the tea and biscuits in the morning that the Queen does not drink or eat. The tea gets cold, the dogs take the biscuits. The Duke goes through to his own dressing room. If the Duke is coming in or going out early, he sleeps in his dressing room. The duty footman is told the night before in which room the tea tray will be required.

Onlookers see a great bond of affection between the Queen and her husband. I saw love. They call each other "darling," as do Prince Charles and Princess Diana, and they mean it.

But they do argue over the funniest things. When Royal retainers are talking together, among the stories always recounted is the one about when the Queen and Prince Philip were in Paris in the early 1970s on a State visit. They were dining alone, except for the inevitable invisible footman and pages, before going on to a reception. The Queen, incidentally, favors receptions rather than grand dinners, as she is less likely to get stuck with somebody desperately boring.

On this occasion a British military regimental band was playing outside. The Duke, listening carefully, said, "Oh, that's my regiment."

"It is not," said the Queen firmly. "It is mine."

And it was. They all are.

This true story causes great amusement in the staff canteen and brings back memories of that other downstairs—apocryphal—joke about the Queen and her brand-new husband standing on the Buckingham Palace balcony after their wedding. Below, the band was playing "God Save the Queen." Her Majesty is supposed to have turned to the newly created Duke of Edinburgh, and said, "Darling, they're playing my tune."

Well, it *is* her tune, along with the law, and the post. It is Her Majesty's Government, Her Majesty's Armed Forces, and Her Majesty's Coastguards. If she liked, she could make everyone a Lord. In theory, she could even declare war. She is highly unlikely to do either.

But though she is not the absolute monarch that her ancestor Queen Elizabeth I was, the Prime Minister is still *her* Prime Minister, and goes in to see her every Tuesday evening at 6:30. In the old days it was always 5:30, but when she became Queen, Prince Charles and Princess Anne were four and two, respectively. She wanted to be with them in the nursery for their bathtime. Indeed, she insisted on being there.

Winston Churchill was the Prime Minister of that day, and she asked him if the time could be changed to an hour later. Readily he obeyed, and from that time on six successive Prime Ministers, including Margaret Thatcher, have arrived at the Palace at half-past-six. On the dot.

As Prince Andrew's address is still officially Buckingham Palace when he is home on leave from his service as a naval helicopter pilot, perhaps his place in this book is here.

Prince Andrew, I'm afraid, has always been a troublemaker since he was a little boy, when I was Nursery Footman. And nothing has changed. He is still trouble, but enormously likable.

I remember him as a small boy who could wreak havoc rather faster than an English football crowd. He was always hitting someone or something, including the unfortunate nursery corgis, poor relations of those close to the Queen. Once, a footman who had had enough hit him back and gave him a black eye. There were no repercussions. The Queen turned a blind eye.

He would go through the dressing-up-box that the Royal children have had for generations and get himself into a cowboy outfit, leaving a trail of disaster behind him. Then he would expect someone else to clean up.

Mabel Anderson, the nanny, would shout at him to put everything away where he had found it. Mutinous, lower lip thrust forward, he would do as he was told. Then, when she wasn't looking, he would take a quick swipe at the corgis to relieve his feelings.

His well-publicized prank of smothering the press with white paint in Los Angeles came as no surprise to me. It was a typical piece of Andrew tomfoolery.

Prince Charles and Prince Andrew don't really get on too well. They have had an odd relationship, with the Prince trying to be big brother and Andrew not responding. I suspect Prince Andrew finds his older brother a little on the stuffy side for his taste.

Prince Charles has never really been difficult in his life; Prince Andrew is most of the time. About four Christmases ago, at Windsor, Prince Andrew was playing up, refusing to send out any Christmas cards or to buy presents for anyone. I suppose he was going through a difficult period, and the Queen asked Prince Charles to have a word with him. Christmas is important to the Queen, a traditionalist down to her toes.

"Speak to him, Charles, and see if you can get him into the family Christmas spirit," she said.

Reluctantly Prince Charles agreed. I don't know what happened, but he came back and made the classic remark that he has always made when thwarted: "I give up," he said.

But the message must have sunk in, because later that afternoon Prince Andrew was seen running around Windsor, with his detective at his heels, shopping.

The Staff don't dislike Andrew, though they do resent him. On Fridays, when the Royal Standard comes down from the flagpole and the Queen is off to Windsor, the Palace goes to sleep. But when Prince Andrew is home on leave, he doesn't want to join the rest of the Royals in the country, which he loathes. He wants to stay in town. This means that the Palace Steward has to keep on a skeleton staff to look after him. There have to be policemen around, a page and a footman are kept to wait on him, and someone stays in the kitchen to see that he is fed, while a housemaid has to be on duty to clean up after him. He has no staff of his own, with the exception of a valet, Michael Perry.

It is rumored that the Queen is doing up a house in the grounds of Kensington Palace for him. If she is, it may be in self-defense. While she was away on tour one time, Prince Andrew took over the nursery. He did it completely off his own bat, deciding he was old enough to have his own independent apartment. He had all the rooms redecorated. The Queen was more than irritated when she came home; it had been quite a costly job. A waste of money, too, since he has now taken over Prince Charles's former rooms, overlooking the Mall.

"Have you told Nanny what you've done?" the Queen asked him when she saw what he had done to the nursery.

"No," he said, obviously thinking that, as Nanny Anderson no longer lived there and had not been there for three years, it hardly mattered to her.

Prince Charles was put out. The nursery was his favorite place. He always went there for his breakfast when Mabel was at the Palace.

There is an awful lot of Edward VII in Prince Andrew. He's indiscreet. He has written a great many letters to Koo Stark, the young American soft-porn actress with whom he took up. He had an affair with an older model, who sold her story and told all. And like his great-great-grandfather before him, he thinks he is God's gift to women. Girls from his own social set were embarrassed when he would put his hands on their knees under the table at dinner parties.

"They were supposed to think they were privileged," one of the Palace staff said, "but those girls don't need that, so now he has turned to showgirls, models and actresses who *do* think they are privileged."

Still, the fact remains that he fought a brave war in the

THE QUEEN, HER HOME, HER HISTORY

Falklands, facing danger equally with his compatriots. There was no special treatment for him because he was the Queen's son. The British public were impressed, and on the strength of that he'll get away with murder for a long time to come.

His brother, Prince Edward, seems quieter, but he too can get into mischief, in a less flamboyant fashion. He was so overshadowed by the powerful personality of Andrew when he was young that I really remember very little about him as a child. I do remember that he loved to help the Queen choose names for the corgi puppies—and that they used the obituary columns of *The Times* to get ideas!

Of course, every family has its problem members, and Royalty are no exception. We used to note, and eventually took for granted, that the Queen Mother and Prince Philip never seem to seek each other out. "Well, they've nothing in common, have they?" one of her staff said one day in the canteen. "She's not intellectual, and he only likes talking to people who are brilliant and stimulating."

This was a pretty accurate assessment. But the Queen Mother and Prince Philip see each other a lot at both formal and family mealtimes. Since they are of equivalent rank, protocol demands that she sits on his right. But that's about it.

Her birthday falls in August. He has never been to the lunch party that she always gives at Clarence House for the celebration. He has a good excuse, of course; it clashes with Royal Cowes Week, a sailing event that he never misses. Princess Anne's birthday also falls in the middle of Cowes Week. Her twenty-first birthday party did not spoil this event; it was held on the yacht.

The Queen had her mother-in-law living with her for some years. Prince Philip's mother, Princess Andrew of Greece, spent the last years of her life at Buckingham Palace. She arrived for good in 1966, a strange old woman in a nun's gray habit. They housed her in the front rooms, where the

Duchess of Windsor stayed when she came to bury the Duke.

It was a curious situation, in a way. Prince Philip had seen little of his mother for many years. She and her husband, Prince Andrew of Greece, had led a turbulent life. They had to flee Greece in the 1914–1918 war when the Greek royal family were at loggerheads with their politicians. They returned to Greece after the end of hostilities, and Prince Philip was born in 1921 on Corfu. Then, when Greece was proclaimed a republic, in 1923, the family had to flee again, to Paris.

They settled there, nearly penniless. Eventually Princess Andrew's brother, Lord Mountbatten, came to the rescue. Having married one of the richest women in Britain, he took the young Prince Philip under his wing and brought him to England. He sent him to Gordonstoun, a tough British school founded on German lines (where Prince Charles was eventually sent). Generally, he turned the boy Philip into the son he had never had.

Lord Mountbatten liked to see himself as a kingmaker, and it was he who engineered the romance between the Queen and his nephew. At first the British were not pleased with the idea of their young Princess marrying a penniless Greek sailor with a title no one had ever heard of. In those days, so soon after the Second World War, the British would have been even more upset if they had been fully aware that Prince Philip has barely a drop of Greek blood. At least, "the Greeks were on our side," as one of the servants who had been at the Palace during the war put it.

Philip's ancestry is partly Danish but, beyond that, almost entirely German. *They* most certainly were not on our side. But he fought a brave war in the British navy, and today everyone in Britain has forgotten all about the early prejudices against him.

Still, perhaps mindful of those early days, his mother was brought into the Palace very quietly. In 1948 she had founded the religious order of Martha and Mary, and was living in seclusion on the Aegean island of Tinos, where she trained nurses. Her health had begun to fail over the years, and she had also run out of money to keep the order going. By 1959 she was staying at the Palace for long periods, and by 1966 she was a permanent resident.

She still wore her nun's habit all the time. She was somewhat eccentric and deaf, and smoked like a chimney. If we could tell when the Queen was coming by the pattering of the corgis' feet, we always knew when Princess Andrew was about from the clouds of smoke that followed her. And the coughing. The poor lady coughed incessantly as she lit another cigarette. Not surprisingly, she was often in the hospital with bronchitis.

Princess Andrew had had a checkered life, though she must have had her moments. Prince Philip was as broke as ninepence when he married Princess Elizabeth; he had little more than his service pay and a few pounds in the bank. So, the big diamond and small stones that made up the Queen's engagement ring came from her mother-in-law. Just as the Queen, in her turn, ordered the Princess of Wales's engagement ring from the Royal Jewelers, Garrard & Company, to Windsor, along with many others, for her to choose her own on the night of the engagement. Princess Diana settled on the biggest!

Princess Andrew had taken her stones to a jeweler on the fourth floor of a block of offices in London's West End, and asked for them to be reset. She never mentioned that the ring was for the future Queen of England. The Queen wears the ring to this day—as I said, it's still an early-warning signal of her irritation when she whizzes it round.

Princess Andrew was a strange but likable old woman. The last years of her life were comfortable. Her presence in the Palace didn't seem to bother the Queen in the least. Bennett and Holloway, the Queen's and the Duke's pages, used to wheel her about in Queen Mary's old wheelchair. (That wheelchair, incidentally, is still about. It is kept and brought out at investitures, in case any of the recipients are handicapped.)

It was the job of Holloway and Bennett to wheel the old Princess in to meals. Said Holloway, "She'd sit there, coughing and smoking, eating nothing but grapes which were specially pipped and peeled for her in the kitchens. She never seemed to eat anything else. But she couldn't half tuck into the wine!"

Considering that Princess Margaret is the only one of the Royals who smokes and how much the rest abhor it, they must have been pretty long-suffering with Princess Andrew. At the end she had two full-time nurses, who had a splendid time choosing anything they wanted to eat from the Palace kitchens. Princess Andrew was by then totally housebound.

When I was Nursery Footman, the small Princes would be taken down to see this other Granny. She was so unlike the Queen Mother; the old lady frightened them a little with her deep voice. But Prince Charles said that when he was older he appreciated her sense of fun and lively mind.

She died in the Palace in December 1969, aged eighty-four. She was buried at Windsor, back where she had been born, a great-granddaughter of Queen Victoria.

Not too much is seen of Prince Philip's relatives these days. There is one week a year, in May, when the Margrave of this and the Baron of that arrive *en masse* for Prince Philip's Windsor Horse Show. They are known by both the Royals and the staff as "the Foreign Relations" and they've become a bit of an embarrassment over the years. All, I suppose, stemming back to the war.

I must say that the Duke was always pleasant to me, though he's not an easy man. There's a restlessness about him, which could come from his unsettled childhood. He never wants to stay in one place for long, except when the family are at Balmoral or Sandringham. He seems content at either place. Going out shooting every day, popping off at the birds, probably takes care of his surplus energy.

On the rare occasions he is in London, he accepts dinner engagements nine times out of ten. The Queen prefers to stay at home in the Palace, which means they almost invariably dine within a mile and a half of each other. If she looks out of her window, she can always see exactly where he is: at the Hilton, the Dorchester, or the Park Lane Hotel, making speeches, helping to raise money for charity. Usually for the National Playing Fields Association, boys' clubs, or the Variety Club of Great Britain.

The Queen will be quite happy at home, watching television. Which is just as well, as she is alone so much. Her husband is constantly on the move. He travels all the time, taking one of the Andovers of the Queen's Flight, or a helicopter. If anyone actually added up the Royals' flying hours, Prince Philip would certainly win hands down. He is, of course, a qualified pilot. A lot of his excess energy was taken up playing polo, but, unfortunately, he has a touch of arthritis and has had to give up that sport. He's now into carriage-driving.

He is obsessed with being manly. The word "macho" could have been coined for the Duke. It's part of his temperament that has caused problems between himself and Prince Charles. Not—let me hasten to say—because Prince Charles is not manly. He most certainly is; but he feels compassion and he can be emotional. He is not a tough, hard person. The Duke has striven to make his son as phlegmatic and unmovable as he himself appears to be, but it has not proved possible.

The Prince does try. On his desk at Kensington Palace he keeps a photograph of himself and his father. It was sent by one of his friends. On it is written *I was not made to follow in my father's footsteps.* Ironically, both are dressed in Trinity House (the Lighthouse Institution) uniforms, the Prince one pace behind his father, but both in the same stance—hand on sword. I think the Prince keeps it in front of him to relish the joke.

I have heard the Duke tell the Prince, in front of guests, and even as recently as since his marriage, "Move your bloody arse!" We were shooting, and he felt Prince Charles was lagging. The Prince never answered back. He just walked off in the opposite direction, looking resigned.

The Duke can't seem to accept that his son has grown up, but it is fair to say that now that Lord Mountbatten has gone, the Prince does go to his father for advice. Ironically, their differing reactions to the appalling death of Lord Mountbatten serve to show up the divisions between them.

I was not with Prince Charles when Lord Mountbatten's body was flown home, nor was I at the funeral. I had been going on holiday, the tickets were booked, and Prince Charles insisted that I go. I have always regretted it.

So the story of the disastrous lunch had to be reported back to me. It took place the day Prince Philip and Prince Charles, along with Lord Rupert Nevill, Prince Philip's Treasurer and Private Secretary, went to Broadlands, Lord Mountbatten's home. They were to go on to Lydd Airport to receive Lord Mountbatten's body, after it had been flown back from Ireland.

Apparently, it was decided that they should eat before leaving, and a light lunch was served. Prince Charles was deeply grieved and barely able to speak. His father was masking his own grief with a brusque and abrupt manner. Much to his father's irritation, Prince Charles held up the serving of lunch by walking down to the River Test, where he used to fish when he stayed with his great-uncle. There he stopped and stood watching the water, composing himself.

I know him in this mood very well. He needs to be alone, away from everyone, so that he can face whatever lies ahead. Prince Philip sent Lord Mountbatten's private secretary, John Barrett, to fetch him, but when John saw the Prince standing there, head bowed, shoulders drooped, he did not have the heart to disturb him. He turned on his heel and went back into the house without doing anything, and told Prince Philip that the Prince would be back shortly.

Eventually Prince Charles reappeared at the table, where his father embarked on a course of baiting his son until the Prince got up and left the table. Both guests and staff in the room found it extremely distressing.

The Duke, I know from experience, was trying to stiffen Prince Charles's backbone for what was to come. I had seen him do it before. But he was wrong then, as he was always wrong in this. The Prince has his own strength in his own way. He does not find it necessary to be bullied.

If the Duke has a motto, it's "Never give up." The trouble is, he doesn't expect anyone else to, either. Take the Royal Yacht: she has had her stabilizers fixed, but the superstructure is so heavy that she wallows like an old tub at times. But the rougher it gets, the happier Prince Philip is, showing everyone he's a man. On that yacht, when it blows it's only Prince Philip and the heroes who are to be found out of their cabins. The Queen herself disappears, quickly and discreetly.

One footman remembers a dreadful night when, on the second night's sailing to an official engagement in Iceland, the ship was struck by a Beaufort scale Force Nine gale. Everyone retired to bed, including all not on duty of the ship's company. Not Prince Philip. He still wanted his dinner, and his poor, unfortunate Equerry, an air force man, had to eat with him. They were served by a page called Mr. Childs and this footman.

There they sat, eating in this vast dining room that can seat sixty all alone. "It was almost impossible to serve," said the footman, "but Mr. Childs had it all worked out. 'Watch for the ship to roll and hang on to the sideboard, old boy,' he said to me, 'and then make a run for it.'

The Queen with Prince Philip, the Duke of Edinburgh, at the State Opening of Parliament, the grandest Royal engagement. She is still carrying her purse, in which she keeps the glasses she needs in order to read her speech. (Syndication International Ltd.)

Diana, Princess of Wales, dressed in shimmering white, joins the Queen in the Irish State Coach on her way to Westminster for the State Opening of Parliament. (Syndication International Ltd.)

The Queen attending a Thanksgiving service. Her Page of Honor is preparing to carry her robes. (© Lionel Cherruault)

The Queen and her corgis leave for Scotland, helped by a footman.
(Press Association Photos)

The Queen wearing some of her fantastic jewelry at a State dinner for President Reagan; the necklace and earrings were made for Queen Victoria's Jubilee. Princess Margaret is on President Reagan's right. (Press Association Photos)

The Queen and Prince Philip in their Highland dress at the Ghillies' Ball, a favorite dance at Balmoral Castle. (Press Association Photos)

*Carriage driving has become Prince Philip's favorite sport since he gave up polo.
(Rex Features Ltd.)*

*The Queen as she likes to be—in comfortable
clothes; she's seen here with Prince Andrew at
horse trials. (Rex Features Ltd.)*

*Royal exercise: the Queen tries to ride every day
except Sunday. (Rex Features Ltd.)*

The Queen rarely drives, except on her own land. She is seen here in her Land-Rover, with her former bodyguard Michael Trestrail in the back seat.
(Rex Features Ltd.)

Although she is the most photographed person in the world, the Queen enjoys taking pictures for the family albums. She is seen here at a polo match.
(Rex Features Ltd.)

Prince Charles shooting, a sport he has given up since his marriage. (Rex Features Ltd.)

Prince Charles fishing in Scotland. (Rex Features Ltd.)

The Prince cuts a dashing figure while playing polo. (© Lionel Cherruault, above, and Mauro Carraro, Rex Features Ltd., below)

"So we hung on to the sideboard, and when the yacht straightened dashed to the table, silver salvers in hand, just in time to cling on to the backs of their chairs while they served themselves.

"The poor old Equerry was getting greener and greener as Prince Philip, never a tidy eater, shoveled food into his mouth, until he had to leave hurriedly. Mr. Childs was all right until Aubrey, the chef, asked if he'd like some rice pudding. Then he had to depart as well."

The difference between Prince Charles and his father is that the younger Prince would never subject anyone to something that caused any distress or discomfort.

We all had the feeling that the Queen rarely interferes between her husband and her eldest son. She is inclined to let them get on with it. She is, of necessity, somewhat detached from motherhood, though she seems to be more maternal than her daughter, Anne, who once said that being pregnant was "an awfully boring time for one." The truth is that it would be impossible to be both the Monarch *and* a doting mother.

Now that Prince Charles has done his duty—married, and given the throne not only one but two heirs—he and the Duke seem to be getting along better. They have a bit more mutual respect. But they could never be totally in accord; their tastes and temperaments are so different.

I had to laugh when we went off to Balmoral on the tail end of the Prince and Princess's honeymoon. They went to a small house, Craigowan, on the estate, where they could have more privacy than in Balmoral Castle itself. When the Prince and Princess arrived at the small, cozy house, they found the walls had all been decorated with the Duke's collection of pictures. Prince Philip has very modern tastes and paints a little himself—not very well—in abstract fashion. Prince Charles's taste is most definitely not modern. He hated the pictures. He sent for me, and commanded that they all be moved to the Staff rooms and the former collection put back. He did it tactfully. He said, "Stephen, could we move these pictures into the Staff rooms? And would the Staff mind swapping theirs back?"

A footman and I removed the modern art, including one of Prince Philip's own efforts—a sort of Balmoral scene—and back on the walls we put all the stags at bay, the Highland scenery and paintings, and sketches of Queen Victoria and her brood. Much more suitable for Craigowan than modern art. "That's better," said the Prince. "Much more in keeping. But no doubt Papa will swap them again at Christmas."

He was right. Next time Prince Philip arrived at the house for the pre-Christmas shoot, perspiring footmen made the change again. And so I suppose it will go on.

There have been earlier conflicts of taste at Balmoral. Queen Victoria had a statue built to her ghillie (*ghillie* is the Scottish word for "gamekeeper"), John Brown, after his death. (Some say he was her lover as well.) The statue stood outside the front door in her lifetime, but after she died her son, Edward VII, promptly had it chucked into the woods. It still stands there, some distance from the house. Life-sized, ivy-overgrown, and horribly lifelike in the dusk, it survives to give the occasional guest a terrible shock.

But back to Prince Philip. His pages are inclined to spend a portion of their lives in a permanent state of perspiration and the remainder doing absolutely nothing. The Prince is away so often that for long periods they are totally without anything to do. Then, when he is there, he works them into the ground, because he himself is so busy, catching up on twice as many engagements as anyone else in half the time. His personal staff get puzzled and paranoid because they see him so rarely, and when they do see him, he seems always to be shouting at them.

In my time he had two valets, both of whom died of heart attacks. A coincidence, of course. His page Bill Holloway, now retired, was a match for anyone and everything, though. He was in the Duke's service for thirty years, a florid chap with a great sense of humor, who would laugh uproariously at his own jokes, but could put on a sober face when on duty.

None of the staff of the period will ever forget the time that Sir Basil Smallpiece, a tycoon of public industry whom the Duke liked, was brought in to modernize the Palace. He decided that time-and-motion-study men should be brought in. It was during one of the periodic economy blitzes, when attempts were made to run the Palace more smoothly and more cheaply.

All of the staff were anxious. Sir Mark Millbank, the Master of the Household, concerned about mounting panic in the senior members of the staff (particularly the Duke's), said no one was to worry: it was just an exercise, to see how Palace procedures could be made more efficient. Indeed, we could all choose when the time-study men would clock our daily routine.

Somehow, they never got around to me. Valets and dressers were left alone. However, Holloway was particularly concerned, because when the Duke was away he had absolutely nothing to do, which, as he said gloomily in the canteen, wasn't "going to look good."

Then he had a stroke of good fortune. He received the news from the Duke's Private Secretary that his boss would be in London for an entire week. Quick as a flash he was off to the time-study people, suggesting they might like to watch him at work.

"I shall be on duty, you see," he said.

Happily for him, they fell for it. For the week that the Duke was home, they zealously recorded everything that Bill did. He, of course, was rushed off his feet; he kept apologizing to them that he simply hadn't time to bring them a sandwich or even a cup of tea. The Duke finally went off again, and the time-study men left Bill in peace. He relaxed into his usual torpor.

The story ended hilariously. When the time-and-motion report was returned to the Palace, it had one particular recommendation: it was felt that Mr. William Holloway, the Duke of Edinburgh's page, required some extra help.

Joe Pearce, one of the valets who died from a heart attack, was working for the Duke while I was with Prince Charles. We were both always being sent things by shops or manufacturers, in the hope that we would persuade our respective bosses to use them and eventually give the makers the chance of getting the Royal Warrant. They were, I'm afraid, wasting their time and their products.

Someone once sent the Prince some aftershave lotion with a sporting name, thinking, I suppose, that he would find it interesting. "Do you want this, sir?" I asked him when it arrived.

He took a sniff. "No, thanks," he said firmly. So I gave it to one of the footmen, who went around wearing it and smelling the Palace out. Usually, though, we put anything that came in into storage. Prince Charles, having inspected it, would say, "That'll keep for Christmas."

Joe was sent an aftershave for Prince Philip, who certainly did not want it. So Joe thought he'd keep it for himself. He slapped it on one morning when he was attending the Duke, and went in to run his bath. The Duke is always grumpy in the morning—well, most of the day, really—and his first words to Joe were, "What's that bloody smell?"

Joe, thinking it might be the drains, opened the windows wide before going out to get the Duke's breakfast. "I can't understand it," said the Duke when Joe came back in, wheeling the trolley. "That smell gets worse."

"I can't smell anything, sir," Joe ventured.

"Well, I can," snapped the Duke.

I was in the pantry dealing with Prince Charles's breakfast

when Joe came in and said, "He's complaining about a smell. I can't smell anything in there."

"Could it be your aftershave?" I asked. Joe had rather overdone it.

"Oh, my God!" he said, and rushed out to try to scrub it off.

One year the Duke took his staff to a Christmas lunch at Madame Prunier's, a fine fish restaurant that used to be in St. James's. At the end of the meal, he got to his feet to make his usual speech of thanks to everyone for their year's hard work. Then he added, "I have a small presentation to make."

All morning Joe had been telling everyone that he had worked for the Duke for twenty-five years. Now he instantly began to preen, ready to get up and take a bow.

"I'd like to thank one of my closest personal staff," the Duke said. Joe was by now almost on his feet as the Duke paused, before saying, "Bill Holloway."

Poor Joe was furious. Bill hadn't, he thought, been around as long as he had or worked so hard. Joe literally died in harness. He was out with Prince Philip and the Queen, shooting, while they were guests at Lord Dalhousie's estate in Scotland.

The Duke and Joe, who was acting as his loader—just as I used to do for Prince Charles—were striding out ahead. The Queen was some way behind, working the dogs, picking up the shot grouse and using binoculars to spot them. Suddenly she saw a figure fall. For one moment she thought it was the Duke; she ran as fast as she could to where the two men were.

Naturally, she was relieved to find that the Duke was perfectly all right, but she was saddened to see Joe Pearce dead. He had been her personal footman when she was Princess Elizabeth, living at Clarence House, so she had known him a long time. And, worse, he was only in his early fifties. His body was taken to Newcastle, in northeast England, where he was buried. The Duke went to the memorial service in St. James's Church in Piccadilly.

Normally, valets retire at sixty, but if the Queen or the Duke takes a shine to anyone, he gets the opportunity to stay on. When the Duke's present page, Mr. Long, reached retirement age, to his surprise the Duke told him, "Don't retire. Stay on as long as you like."

Long was delighted. He has had a heart condition for years, and cannot carry anything heavy. Staying on suited him very well, though it did not please younger staff hoping for promotion. Because of the Duke's frequent absences and with his having his own married quarters, Long was paid and could still go out to do catering jobs for a bit of extra pin money. But, then, all the staff do this, as the Palace pay is not good. A page earns about £120 a week; a footman about £80. Therefore the staff are always to be found earning a bit on the side at the Finnish embassy, who don't seem to have any staff of their own.

The Queen and the Duke don't mind these extramural activities, so long as it does not affect their own comfort. In fact, it sometimes enhances it. The Queen once turned up at a dinner at one of the livery companies in London, to find that her chef had cooked the meal—at least she was certain of a good dinner. And the Household, who are always going to receptions and city guild parties, are quite relieved when they find the Palace pages and footmen in attendance. It means they will be looked after and never left without a drink in their hands—a good-sized one at that.

I was surprised that the Queen was aware that someone from the Palace was cooking that night. She must be the only person in the country who never sees her chef. She has a menu book brought to her by her page every morning, and she just crosses off what she doesn't want served for the day.

If there are any problems with the kitchen, it is always the

Duke who goes to sort it out. He seems to be more interested in food than the Queen is. Not that he eats a great deal. Neither of them does.

They do each have favorite puddings, in both cases made with chocolate. Prince Charles absolutely loathes chocolate puddings, and can hardly bring himself to eat them. Perhaps he had too many as a child. The Queen's favorite, which she firmly believes she invented herself, is homemade ice cream with very expensive Bendick's chocolate chipped into it. She calls it her Dalmatian pudding. No one has had the heart to tell her that it has been going for donkeys' years overseas in the United States as chocolate chip ice cream.

The Duke loves a chocolate mousse made with Glenfiddich malt whisky. The funny old cook-housekeeper they had at one of the old Scottish houses used to make this to perfection. One night when the Duke, Prince Charles, and Princess Anne were up in Scotland for the pre-Christmas shoot, the Duke ordered the mousse for the next day.

Breakfast is served in the dining room, not in the bedrooms. When they came down the next morning they found the old girl kneeling, rolling out the pastry for the lunchtime pie on the floor, the mousse finished, and an empty Glenfiddich bottle rolling at her side. We'd always known she drank like a fish. She used to "rev" down to Ballater on an old motorbike if she wanted anything, but everyone put up with her, because it was so hard to find someone to work in the depths of a freezing Scottish winter.

The Duke thought it was very funny at the time; at least it gave him and his guests something to talk about over dinner that night. But three days later, after Christmas, she was sent for by the Master of the Household, and sacked.

The Royals enjoy it when the staff do something eccentric, but then common sense takes over, and the Master has to do the dirty work of firing employees. The old girl probably assumed she had got away with it, but the family would not have wanted to fire her over Christmas.

Years ago, the Duke once asked John Dean, his valet at the time, "John, where's my jacket?"

The valet said, "I presumed you'd helped yourself, sir."

"Don't ever presume anything," said the Duke. "Find my jacket."

Never to presume is not a bad rule for anyone in Royal service.

Chapter Four

TABLE TALK

A STATE BANQUET AT BUCKINGHAM PALACE IS PROBABLY ONE of the most splendid and awe-inspiring sights in the world. For sheer grandeur, only a great public occasion, like a coronation or a Royal wedding, can beat it.

A State banquet, in all its formal, glittering glory, was also the setting for one of the funniest sights I have ever seen, an unfortunate but hilariously comic sequence of events that I still treasure.

State banquets take place in the Ballroom of Buckingham Palace, and a fortunate few are allowed to watch the proceedings from behind a carefully camouflaged grille set at the far end of the Ballroom. Serving members of the Palace Staff can apply for tickets for relatives or friends to watch unseen. And Staff who are off duty can watch as well.

The grille is there for people to look through, not for security. Yeomen of the Guard stand around the room, pikes in hand, to ensure the safety of the Monarch and her guests. The Captain of the Guard, in plumed helmet, strides around the banquet table all through the proceedings. I'd usually go down and have a look myself, particularly when Prince Charles was present. Just in case he might need something.

The Archbishop of Canterbury is generally invited to these State banquets, and on this night he was seated, as usual, near the Queen. The guest opposite the Archbishop was a Dame Commander of the Order of the British Empire, who was also a full brigadier in the army. I'm not sure, but she could have been the highest-ranking woman in the service.

A large and handsome lady, she had a bosom of splendid proportions, and wore a black evening dress held up with thin shoulder straps. Across the left side of her dress were pinned a galaxy of ribbons and orders. Women from the services generally prefer to wear a dress rather than a uniform to State banquets, and ribbons, rather than the medals themselves, are worn.

The Staff waiting at the tables are in full livery—acres of velvet shot through with miles of gold thread. On the sleeves of these ornate uniforms are five large gilt buttons, emblazoned with the Queen's coat-of-arms.

I had noticed the fine female form of the lady brigadier while I was standing behind the grille. It would have been hard to miss her. The hors d'oeuvres had been served, and I watched the Queen give the Palace Steward the signal to remove the plates used in this course and bring on the next.

As the young footman assigned to the Dame Commander's section bent over to serve her some broccoli, the gilt buttons on his jacket became entangled in the ribbons on her left bosom.

He had a problem extricating himself. Finally, he set down the silver dish of broccoli—not easy on a table laden with gold plate, crystal, and fine china. Somehow, with a little help from the Dame Commander—who commendably kept her head—the footman, now as scarlet as his jacket, managed to untangle himself. Visibly relieved, he leaned over to pick up his broccoli and maneuver the gilt buttons past the Dame Commander's ribbons, when disaster struck again.

Unfortunately for him, one button had caught in the shoulder strap of her evening gown.

This time the lady panicked. Dismayed, she pulled away from him; in a state of nervous embarrassment, he pulled the other way. The result was inevitable. The shoulder strap snapped in two.

Her face horrified, the lady pushed herself back from the table. The movement also pushed her out of her not-quite-sufficiently-ample bodice. Guests in her vicinity were riveted. So was I. From behind the safety of the screen, I was rolling with laughter. The Archbishop took one look and modestly inspected his place. The Queen never missed a beat in her conversation with the visiting head of state, the President of Austria. He, though, seemed to have his mind more on what was going on than on what the Queen had to say.

The footman, again minus his broccoli, which had slipped from his grasp, made a vague snatch in the direction of the two ends of the shoulder strap, gave up, and retreated. He was closely followed by the brigadier, who, holding her dress together with one hand, had mustered an amazing amount of dignity under the circumstances.

Dinner resumed its stately pace. It is much to the credit of the army that, returning after a quick repair involving a safety pin, the lady settled back at the table, smiling and talking as if nothing had happend.

Such diversions are rare at a State banquet. Everything is so carefully planned that it is unusual for anything to go wrong. But even without topless lady brigadiers, these banquets are something to behold. There are always over a hundred guests, seated around a vast horseshoe table. The Queen and her guest of honor are placed at the head of the table, below the dais that holds twin thrones. These thrones, set under a huge, ornate canopy, were built for the visit of King George V and Queen Mary to India in 1911. As Emperor and Empress, they were seated on them to receive the homage of the Indian princes at the Great Delhi Durbar. The thrones were brought back to England, and have been at the Palace ever since. These beautiful gilt-and-velvet chairs dominate even a setting as vast as a table sometimes laid for one hundred and fifty magnificently dressed people.

The laying of the table is itself a theatrical event. Underbutlers do the work, supervised by the Palace Steward. Every solid gold knife and fork is measured for distance with a ruler before it is put into place, so that the cutlery is in perfect symmetry. The youngest and lightest of the underbutlers gets up on the table, wearing soft slippers rather like airline socks. He walks down the center of the table, carefully placing each piece of crystal glass, and making certain that the huge silver candelabra are equidistant from each other. The same pattern is followed when State banquets are held at Windsor, as one was for President Reagan and his wife. But at Windsor the banquet is held in St. George's Hall, a superb room redesigned by George IV in the early nineteenth century.

Hundreds of years of tradition go into the pageantry of this dining spectacle unmatched in all the world. If a State banquet in the 1980s does not quite compare with the nine courses and forty-five separate dishes served as a matter of routine during the reign of Queen Victoria, this probably comes only as a considerable relief to the guests.

Today, in a diet-conscious world, though the Royal decor has not changed, food is much simpler. A typical Buckingham Palace State banquet begins with soup, either consommé or a crème Saint-Germain. A fish dish will follow, the choice depending on the season—perhaps a small portion of lobster, or salmon mousse. These will be dressed with perfectly made sauces.

The Queen is fond of rack of lamb, and more often than not, this will be served as the main course. Game is never on the menu, as the Queen feels that some guests may not enjoy it. Meat is always garnished with three or four vegetables, brought straight from the market. Then follows salad, in the French manner. The dessert will be cold, as so many people have to be served. And predictable. It will be some kind of ice cream or bombe turned out of a mold. Five different wines of outstanding quality are served throughout the meal.

Cheese is never served at dinner, even privately. Fruit, which has been decorating the table in superb gold dishes, will then be removed and served to the guests. Coffee and petits fours follow. These are served in icing sugar baskets, decorated with ribbons in the national color of the guest country.

The Lord Chamberlain calls for silence. The Queen pops on her spectacles to read her speech. Responses are made, and then the Royal party and all the guests proceed to other drawing rooms for coffee and liqueurs and—much to the relief of those who want to smoke—cigars and cigarettes. There is no smoking at the table at a State banquet.

Those invited are chosen from every walk of life. There is usually a sprinkling of business tycoons, film and theater people, and sports figures chosen to lighten the mix of politicians and members of the three armed services who predominate. Conversation is intelligent and subdued. The guests make a discreet buzz, while music is provided by the string section of one of the Royal regimental bands.

The only drawback to these glittering occasions is that the men must wear white tie and tails, garments both Prince Charles and Prince Philip loathe.

When Prince Charles saw me getting his clothes together in his bedroom for one of these evenings, he would look at me and say, "Oh! Bloody white tie!" And the air would be Royal Blue as he struggled to dress himself.

TABLE TALK

The Ballroom is the only room at Buckingham Palace big enough for a banquet, but unfortunately the kitchens are some distance away. Over the years, a system of traffic lights has been developed, so that members of Staff serving the guests always know where they should be and exactly what they should be doing. The traffic lights are hidden, of course —placed behind the thrones. A red light means that the course just served is proceeding as it should be, and Staff can stand still for a moment. The amber light warns them to be ready to begin clearing the table between courses. And the green light means, as you might guess, go get the next course. The traffic lights are controlled by the Palace Steward. Mr. Dickman, from his station behind the Queen's chair.

When the light turns green, dozens of footmen—and I used to be among them—leap into action. The taller ones are always chosen to serve around the horseshoe end of the table—they can reach across the spaces more easily. I was very young when I served at a couple of these banquets and therefore worked far down the table. The seniors always look after the top table and the important people. Staff at the Palace enjoy the banquets, though they are hard work. They bring out all the finest traditions of Royalty and show how efficient the system can be. It sometimes puzzles visitors that the Royal Family never wait for everyone to be served. As soon as their plates are in front of them and full, they start eating. You can hardly blame them, as food doesn't take long to get cold. It will already have traveled about half a mile to get to the table, then will have been sitting on a hotplate outside the room waiting to be served.

The Household end of the table is served last, after the guests. They have to eat as fast as they can to catch up. I often used to wonder why they did not all have permanent indigestion.

In the old days, as soon as the King put down his knife

and fork, his page, who always stands behind the Monarch, would immediately clear away. That was a signal for every other plate on the table to be taken away, willy-nilly, regardless of whether or not the diner had finished eating.

The Queen has not exactly ended this custom, but conjured a way around it. She looks carefully around the table —no matter whether it is a State banquet or a smaller, more intimate meal—and checks on her guests' progress. She herself eats frugally, and she will often have finished before anyone else. But she has a small salad on a side plate, and she toys with this until the rest of the guests have caught up. But once she finally puts down her fork, it's all systems go.

Prince Charles is the slowest of the Royal eaters. He'll be chatting away and fiddling with his food, when suddenly he'll feel his father's glaring eye on him. Then he quickly puts down his knife and fork.

It is a daunting thought that the Queen attends an average of sixty State lunches and dinners, plus three banquets, every year. Prince Philip presides at nearly ninety. Prince Charles, in my day, while often joining the Queen and Prince Philip, also held his own functions in the Chinese Dining Room, a splendid room, if like a rather superior Chinese restaurant.

So the potential for Royal boredom is considerable. Maybe it is because they become so fed up with these endless meals that some of them have terrible manners. The Duke of Edinburgh gobbles his food as if he can't get rid of it fast enough. He has been known to put fastidious eaters right off their meals! Lord Mountbatten used to mash everything on his plate into nursery food.

The late Duke of Gloucester died of Parkinson's disease. Though he led as normal a life as possible, mealtimes were not easy for anyone. When he was trying to eat his soup, the whole table was agog, waiting for him to get something into his mouth. The Queen was marvelous with him, enormously patient. She ate extremely slowly herself, so as not to embarrass him.

I can't remember now what brought the subject up, but Prince Charles once regaled me with stories of his Great-Uncle Harry, the Duke of Gloucester. He and his Duchess, Princess Alice, used to join the Royals for summer at Balmoral, where dinner each night was formal. The ladies wore long dresses and their jewelry; the men, if they were entitled to do so, wore the kilt. All the Royal Family have the right to wear the Royal Stuart tartan. And it is true that Scotsmen wear nothing under their kilts.

"When the ladies joined the gentlemen after dinner," Prince Charles told me, "all the men would be sprawled around, and Princess Alice's shout of 'Knees, Harry!' would reverberate around the drawing room. The Duke would then smartly snap his knees together. Usually too late."

The Royals to this day still have the ladies retire after dessert is served. The men, like men everywhere, tell their risqué stories over the port and cigars, while the ladies powder their noses. At a big dinner they like the custom because it means that if they've been stuck with someone boring for the past two hours, at least in the drawing room they can jockey for a better partner.

The late King used to love sitting over dinner, and, once the port was being passed, he and the other gentlemen would stay for hours after the ladies had retired. He and his Queen never drank coffee—always tea—in the drawing room. When she thought he had been away quite long enough, she would draw a teapot on a piece of paper and say to her page, "Take that to His Majesty." And he, who adored his wife, would be in the drawing room in a flash.

Dinner is served at Balmoral at 8:15. If it is informal, it is usually followed by one of the latest movies, shown in the ballroom, which doubles as a cinema. Occasionally, weather permitting, a barbecue will be arranged. But generally the dinners are formal.

A Royal barbecue consists of lots of steaks, sausages, chops, and all kinds of salads that are prepared in the Royal kitchens. Wine is served as well as beer, for those who want it. All the food and drinks are kept in a special carrier, designed by Prince Philip, which has separate refrigerated sections and hot sections. The Royals themselves like to do the cooking on the big coke-fired barbecue, but they do not do the washing up!

The Staff are not too keen on barbecues; more often than not, something has been forgotten, and—since this is usually held some distance from the house—a lot of running backwards and forwards for the napkins or the tongs is involved. I remember once the coke for the grill was forgotten, and Prince Philip was furious because he couldn't get on with cooking the meal.

There are about fourteen guests at a time invited to Balmoral or Sandringham. The Queen arranges the seating plan. She works from a list of the guests made up the night before and moves them around so that eventually everyone gets a turn with a Royal dinner partner. She and Prince Philip sit at the center of the table, facing each other. The Household are always at either end.

Since the Queen travels with her own chef and kitchen staff, the standard of the food is consistently high. The Royals eat four times a day—breakfast, lunch, tea, and dinner, though the main meal is at night. In the country, picnics are a more likely lunchtime choice.

As with the rest of us, at a Royal picnic, the food is cold. Cold game, egg dishes, cold meats, lots of salads. Practical rather than fancy; easy to eat with a fork out of plastic containers. Out on the moors, the silver is left at home.

Dinner is rather grander, and always by candlelight glowing from four-stemmed candelabra. The Queen and lady guests wear long dresses and fine jewelry. The men will be in black tie and, in Scotland, will sometimes wear the kilt. The food is served by liveried footmen, with the Yeoman of the Cellars pouring first-class wine.

Dinner is never more than four courses. A usual menu would be scampi, game from the Estates, salad, and either a sweet or a soufflé before coffee is served. In Scotland, the Queen's Pipe Major enters after coffee, and strides around the table playing the bagpipes, just as he does every morning outside the Queen's bedroom window.

The aristocracy are not above a bit of meanness. While dinner at Balmoral is ample, it is not lavish—not unreasonably, since everyone has usually eaten an enormous lunch.

One of the regular guests at Balmoral is the Duchess of Grafton, who also happens to be the Queen's Mistress of the Robes. Her job is to attend the Queen on important occasions, like the opening of Parliament. One evening the Duchess was still a little peckish after the meal was finished. She made the mistake of trying to secrete a bunch of grapes in her handbag. The Queen's eagle, all-seeing eye spotted her, and to this day the Duchess is teased about her little bit of "tablelifting." The grapes would certainly have come out from the kitchen again to be served the next evening. These days there is little waste in the Palace kitchens—yet another modern innovation that the older staff deplore.

In the old days, before the economies were really imposed, there was an under-butler called Mitchell at Windsor. He lived in the grounds of the Castle. For lunch at least four chops would be cooked for each guest. Most people took only two, or three at the most. If the page didn't get there first, Mitchell would borrow one of the picnic hotboxes, and within twenty minutes of the Queen's having eaten her lunch, Mitchell's wife and children would be having the same meal down at the cottage where he lived.

A lot of food is recycled now, and it still comes hard to Prince Charles to throw anything away. At Highgrove,

Prince Charles's country home, we always had a fridge full of moldering bits and pieces that we'd finally eat up in some frightful concoction rather than have any waste. Now the Princess is slowly getting the Prince to accept the idea that, even in the best regulated households, some food is always going to wind up in the garbage pail.

When it comes to food, they are a predictable family. They always eat the same thing on Sundays: roast beef with the British trimmings of Yorkshire pudding and baked potatoes. Pudding is always *crème brûlée* and peaches. Easter Sunday it has to be boiled eggs for breakfast—another British tradition, like the roast beef on Sunday. Year after year, Michael Sealey, the chef, used to make all sorts of fancy suggestions for Easter breakfast. They were all crossed out and "boiled eggs" firmly written on the menu book.

Considering that none of the Royals is overweight, some of them eat an awful lot. When they go shooting at Sandringham in the winter, they start lunch with hot food. This will generally be a stew, or chicken in cream sauce, or a beef casserole. After they've polished off the hot dish a cold collation of ham, tongue, or beef is served. Then there's dessert, usually a good rib-sticking sponge, followed by cheese. These meals are held in various church halls or Boy Scouts' meeting places, scattered around the estate.

Staff get exactly the same meal. I used to look forward enormously to lunch when I was trudging around loading for the Prince on these shooting expeditions. The food was first-class and welcome.

I remember one Boxing Day shoot (Boxing Day is the day after Christmas) when we were all at Windsor. The guns go out at 9:30, then, at about eleven, the Staff leave to set up the luncheon. This time it was in a little hall in the middle of the Home Park. The building hadn't been used since the previous year, and the footmen had to do a massive clean-up, sweeping, washing, and dusting before it was even remotely habitable.

TABLE TALK

They then set up the table with linen, silver, glass, and china, all brought from the Castle. They had towels and soap for the lavatories. They were thinking that everything looked okay—until one of the footmen went into the ladies' loo to leave hand towels. To his horror, the walls were covered with the most unbelievable graffiti. Obscene drawings and four-letter words—nothing the Royal ladies should see! Someone was dispatched post-haste back to the Castle to bring bleach and cleansing materials. They had a good try, but they couldn't get everything off the walls by the time the Royal party arrived at the hall for lunch.

The Queen Mother appeared first, had a drink, and then said she thought she would wash her hands. She disappeared into the lavatory, and it seemed to the footman that she was there rather a long time. She finally emerged without the faintest trace of expression. Then all the Royal ladies appeared—the Queen, Princess Margaret, the Kents, the Gloucesters. Each in turn headed off to wash her hands, followed by their lady guests.

They must have thought the footmen were mad. Every time anyone went in and came out, the men's heads were on swivels to see if there was any reaction. But no sign did the ladies give, either of amusement or shock. They just drank their aperitifs and settled down to eat.

Even in a broken-down village, on a shooting lunch the same rules apply as at the Palace. The Queen's footman, the Duke's footman, and other footmen will be there. As in the private dining rooms of all the Royal residences, the Royals are never alone when they eat. Along with footmen, the pages will be there, and someone from the silver pantry, another from the glass and china, plus under-butlers acting as waiters and commis (or junior) waiters.

The family take absolutely no notice of Staff, and in the end, Staff take absolutely no notice of them. But it is difficult at first. I remember I stared most rudely, trying my hardest not to, when I first saw the Queen about two feet away from me. The same thing happens to everyone in Royal service until they become inured.

We had a great problem with one footman. He finally had to be removed from table duties, simply because he had fallen in love with Princess Margaret. He couldn't take his eyes off her.

As a footman, once you've done your bit at the table you retreat backwards, lean against the wall, stare at the ceiling or the carpet, and generally make yourself scarce. This poor footman stood and stared at the Princess with cowlike devotion. It nearly drove her mad; so eventually they placed him so that he was standing behind her. This was no improvement.

"She can feel his eyes boring into her back," Prince Charles said to me. Finally they were forced to find him a different job. But he isn't alone. Footmen are introduced gently into the dining room for this very reason. It is all carefully done, and only when you're completely comfortable in the Royal presence do you become senior and actually get to serve them.

I remember a young footman, a Lancashire lad. The first time he was really close to the Queen, he was standing holding eight magnificent dessert plates. At the sight of her he turned bright scarlet and dropped the lot. Every single one of them was smashed.

"Don't worry," the Queen said immediately. "Just carry on."

It was, I thought, remarkably long-suffering of her, as each plate was worth well over £100. But breakages are not too much of a tragedy in the Palace. They own such superb china, and so much of it, that each course is served on a different service. Some of these services go back to many earlier reigns. One is from Queen Alexandra's dowry—a Flora Danica of fine Danish bone china that she brought to

Britain with her when she came to marry the future Edward VII. It is still in regular use at Sandringham, and must be worth a fortune today.

The Palace and the Queen's other homes are full of beautiful china, but when they are dining privately, the food served on it is simple in the extreme. They never eat more than two courses when they are *en famille* and generally of something light. The food is, of course, first-class and most beautifully cooked, but in small quantities.

Princess Diana and Prince Charles will almost always eat a piece of fish, probably salmon, or will just have a simple soufflé—the Princess's favorite dish. Prince Charles likes chicken vol-au-vent, but rarely eats any other kind of meat. Princess Diana has a passion for potatoes baked in their jackets. Mixed salads, using every conceivable ingredient, are always served. The food is brought in on a hot trolley and they prefer to serve themselves.

There was a time, when I first went to the Palace, when even if the Queen was eating alone—which she frequently does, particularly at lunchtimes—a whole flock of Staff were in attendance. Now she, too, serves herself from the hot-plate, though her footman is never far away.

For these less formal occasions, the Queen prefers plain white china with a band of color around the edge, though this won't do for State occasions or formal dinner parties. Then she uses the most amazing gold plates with the Royal crest—the shield, the lion, and the unicorn—engraved into them. For the less important meals, there are dozens of different patterned chinas to choose from, and the Queen uses them in rotation. They are mostly Victorian, made by Sèvres and the best of the British porcelain craftsmen. In Scotland the favorite service has thistles around the edge of the plates. This was specially created for Queen Victoria. A superb collection of Waterford crystal, which was specially commissioned by George III, is also kept at Balmoral, though this is rarely used now. The Queen still has Queen Victoria's linen table napkins; these are so big that they are used as tray cloths these days.

All the "cut" glass—which in the normal way is made by Brierley—has the *E.R.* engraved into it, for "Elizabeth Rex." This glass is not used for really big gatherings. Then the ordinary caterer's glass comes out.

Appropriately all the solid silver cutlery is in King's pattern. All the white, crisply starched linen has the Royal monogram woven in.

Much of the china has been damaged over the years by Staff, which is not really surprising, as everything is still washed by hand. The only electric dishwasher that the Royal Family owns is at Sandringham because it was decided that they would cut down on servants and install labor-saving gadgets. Everyone would "muck in."

The entire time I worked for the Royal Family my heart used to sink when the suggestion that we would all "muck in" was raised.

We were all going to "muck in" at Highgrove when the Prince first bought it, and he, his detective, and I went down for weekends. Mucking in consisted of the detective suddenly finding that he had an awful lot of important phone calls to make and the Prince nodding off over the television, while I was out in the kitchen cooking supper. And serving it. And washing up. And getting breakfast.

There was a lot of mucking in when the Prince was first married, too. As newlyweds, they didn't want too many people about when they went to Highgrove, so it was suggested that we all muck in—with much the same result.

Having served the meal, I would retire to my room. At about 11:30, the Princess would knock on my door and say in dulcet tones, "We've finished, Stephen. You can come and clear away now."

Mucking in at Sandringham was supposed to mean that even the Royals carried their own luggage. Needless to say, it never happened. All that did occur was the advent of the dishwasher and the turning of the fine old-fashioned kitchens into a tiled hygienic monstrosity. Go through the swing doors now, and you could be in a municipal canteen. The kitchen has lost all its character. There's no copper on the walls anymore, nothing cozy. And yet the Royals are frightfully proud of it; the Duke is always showing visitors around his fine new kitchen.

Still, the dishwasher may help the china survive, provided that it doesn't remove all the decoration. The glasses still have to be washed by hand. As the years go by, the value of what the family owns in fine china, crystal, and silver increases.

The Staff, generally speaking, don't mind taking responsibility for all these beautiful things. It's amazing how the people who work in the glass and silver pantries begin falling in love with the stuff they look after. They start treating each item as their own. It happens a lot. The housemaids become very possessive of their territory, particularly the old brigade, guarding their rooms and getting quite uppity if anyone encroaches on what they feel is their area.

For many years all the gilt plate and table ornaments, cruets, and so on were kept in a large storeroom just inside the Palace, near the trade door. Within fifty yards of the Royal Mews was a glass cupboard full of priceless stuff. Though I gather not as much as there used to be. Prince Charles told me that an awful lot of the plate had been melted down by his mad ancestor, the Duke of Connaught.

When Hardy Roberts came to the Palace as the new Master of the Household, he could not believe that all anyone ever needed was a big key to get at these Palace treasures. He promptly had the whole lot moved to the cellars and stored in what had been an old air-raid shelter, now made into a vault. He had an elevator put in. Now all the gold is in a strongroom, with an alarm wired up to the Palace police station.

In the old days, when I first went to the Palace, if anyone

had family visitors, all you had to do was approach the old Yeoman of the Plate. If he liked you, he'd open the door with the one key and let anyone have a look around. There it all was—gold plates, silver plate, knives, forks, huge candelabra, table-centers, cruets, serving dishes and family heirlooms, glittering like Aladdin's cave before your very eyes.

But over the years some things have been lost. The spoons were the worst; people stole them for souvenirs all the time. Now, for everyday catering, they've bought ordinary ones, so that people don't bother to take them anymore.

Cutlery is a tempting souvenir. But the one thing no one would be able to steal from the Royals are fish knives and forks. The Royals never use them, believing them to be frightfully middle-class, if not "common."

Today, after a banquet or a dinner, when the good stuff comes back to the silver pantry, it's all counted. But this is only recent. In the old days, we just used to leave everything until the morning, wash up, and then put it away.

Staff can still borrow glasses if they are having guests, but not with quite the ease we all did before Hardy Roberts arrived. Everything has become much more organized over the years, and it is not as happy and easygoing a place to work in as it used to be.

Hardy Roberts was quite a one for change. The first year he was there, he noticed that at the Queen's Staff Ball— which is always held at Christmas in Buckingham Palace— the mixture was a bit odd. Everyone was allowed to bring a guest, but it seemed to him that there were a great many more men guests than there should be. He issued a directive the following year that gentlemen staff must bring only lady guests.

The older staff who have been there many years talk with great nostalgia of times past. Some have been there most of their adult lives. Walter Fry, the old Yeoman of the Plate who was so generous with the key to the gold, had many stories to tell. He had worked for the Duke of Windsor for the brief time when he was King Edward VIII, before Mrs. Simpson came on the scene.

"Terrible table-manners, that woman had," Walter used to say. "I'd be standing there, waiting for her to serve herself and holding this huge silver entrée dish of vegetables. She'd be talking. Whoever she was talking to was aware of this great steaming heavy dish, and they'd be embarrassed. Not her.

"We fixed her," said Walter. "She'd usually come out from dinner with a burn on her shoulder. Well, we had to give her a gentle nudge before we dropped the lot, didn't we?"

But, as Walter pointed out, Mrs. Simpson's lack of concern for the staff would often cause them to have burns on their hands, too. Silver and gilt retain the heat.

"Very painful to handle, it is," Walter would say.

Another inconsiderate hostess is Princess Michael of Kent. She gives superb dinner parties, but can't really afford permanent staff, so she borrows. Mr. Bennett, whom I've mentioned before, with his grace-and-favor apartment in Kensington Palace, is a sort of neighbor to her (though, as might be expected, her apartment is considerably grander than his). As he lives so close, she often asks him to butle for her.

One night she was serving soup, and had it put into an enormous silver tureen. Bennett took one look at the size of it and put soup cups around and found a silver soup ladle. He planned to fill the cups from the tureen and serve them to the guests on a separate tray.

"No! No!" cried the Princess when he started to fill the individual cups. "Bring the tureen around, please."

Bennett did as he was bid, giving each guest a cup and then carting the tureen and ladle round the table. He nearly ruptured himself, and it is said he hasn't been back since.

At least Princess Michael is genuinely interested in food, which is more than you can say for the rest of the Royal

Family. Prince Philip takes more interest than most, but he really only complains when the food is not to his taste. The others barely notice. For years the Duke used to cook his own breakfast of bacon and eggs in his own room in an electric frying pan. Today he doesn't eat cooked breakfast, being on a health kick: now it's yogurt, bran, and nuts and fruit.

And it was Prince Philip who one day introduced a funny little give-away cookbook into the kitchens. Produced and given away free by a Scottish company who make canned food and preserves, it is now the Royal food bible. Much to the frustration of the chefs.

The Royal chefs are pretty good. All three are properly trained—they even sent the Deputy Head Chef off to Switzerland for more experience. Another trained for a while at the Capital Hotel in Knightsbridge—one of those small, secret hotels that produce exquisite food. It seems hardly worth the bother, but, then, in their public life the Royals are constantly faced with Cordon Bleu cooking. Light food must come as a relief.

Now the canning company's little free book has its recipes tried out at Craigowan, or Balmoral, or Wood Farm at Sandringham. If the results are acceptable, the recipe goes into the Royal menu book. The recipes are certainly not for State occasions, but they're good, stick-to-the-ribs dishes designed for open-air people.

But, as I say, *haute cuisine* is not their scene, though Princess Diana has cheered things up a bit. She likes delicate fish and soufflés, in fact prefers her food to be hot, whereas Prince Charles really likes cold food best.

Something I have fond memories of is the nursery tea in the Palace, back in the days when I was Nursery Footman. Prince Andrew and Prince Edward were little then, and on Sunday afternoons the Palace coffee ladies would make us all jam pennies for our tea. These were jam sandwiches made from Elsenham jam, and cut with a round pastry cutter into circles. Why that shape should have tasted better I don't know, but they did. And the children loved them. No crusts to eat up. The coffee ladies who made the jam pennies are an institution at the Palace. There are four of them, employed only to make coffee, starting with grinding the beans fresh and then brewing in old-fashioned earthenware pots.

I once worked out that it probably cost the Palace £20,000 a year just to make a good cup of coffee—once you started adding up the coffee ladies' insurance, pensions, and housing. They work in what would be called a stillroom at a hotel. At the Palace, it's the coffee room. The four ladies are rarely busy, except at the summer garden parties where they work extremely hard, providing all the Royal tea and sandwiches for the Royal guests. The masses milling around the lawns get Joe Lyons, a down-market catering company.

The ladies are not responsible for making the cakes or buns that go with mid-morning or afternoon coffee. There is yet another kitchen for this called the Royal Pastry, where these are baked and then taken to the coffee room. The Royal Pastry also makes ice cream, simple Victoria jam sponges, biscuits, and sometimes a chocolate cake, plus all the dessert mousses and the Royals' great favorite—crêpes suzette. They make flans, according to the fruit in season, and also soufflés—cheese, lemon, or Grand Marnier–flavored. They also dress the fruit bowls and squeeze the orange juice for breakfast.

There is a set routine. The coffee ladies make coffee for all the breakfast trays. Since the coffee room is near the Palace kitchens, the coffee is not very hot when it arrives. It is fair to say that Muriel Tate, who for four years ran the coffee room, made the most wonderful brew. Queen Frederika of Greece always used to say that she came to Balmoral only for the coffee. She drank gallons of the stuff.

The coffee ladies do get to travel. They move around with the Court to Windsor and Balmoral. But not to Sandringham. Because that's where we all muck in!

Chapter Five

THE WALES FAMILY

LADY DIANA ALWAYS USED TO SAY IN THE EARLY DAYS OF HER courtship with Prince Charles that she wanted at least four children.

This was in the days when she was working at a nursery school and I was sneaking her out the back door of her flat, helping her dodge the press, and whisking her off to visit Prince Charles in either her own Mini-Metro or one of the Palace cars. I thought at the time it was just as well that she was a lover of children, as the most important thing that the wife of the heir to the throne can do is to ensure the continuance of the Royal line.

This she has most certainly done, with not just one but two bonny sons. She has the irrepressible William, who is a little terror, inclined—as both the Prince and Princess admit

—to be "destructive." And now the new young Prince Henry, who was born on September 15, 1984.

Having been working for the Prince throughout the early days of the Princess's pregnancy with William, I had a feeling she would put off having another baby for a while. She most certainly did not enjoy being pregnant: she used to mutter that if men had the babies, there wouldn't be any. But she does love the end result of the morning sickness and the not fitting into her fashionable clothes. She genuinely enjoys being a mother, which, sadly, does sometimes cause friction in a lifestyle where children are basically left to Nanny's care while Mother is a public figure, out performing Royal engagements.

Prince Charles is rather caught between two stools in the matter of bringing up the children. He used to say to me that he would never want to inflict the kind of schooling he had on any child. He loathed being at Gordonstoun, the tough "outward bound"–style school in Scotland that his father chose for him. He was desperately miserable there, and it is pretty certain that neither William nor Henry will become pupils there when they are old enough.

As a very little boy he also found going to his junior school something of an ordeal. He was constantly photographed and could not help but be the odd child out. Prince Charles was the first heir to the throne to actually *go* to school—his mother was educated by a governess in the Palace, and I wonder if he will want to subject his own sons to the pressure that he felt when he was pushed out into the real world.

How the Royal Princes are educated will, in the end, probably depend on Princess Diana. She is definitely the one who makes the decisions about what happens to the children, and already she has broken through generations of Royal protocol.

For example, the Queen never arrived at the nursery unannounced when her children were small. I remember when

I was Nursery Footman and we knew the Queen was coming to see Prince Andrew and Prince Edward, there was great fuss and bother to make sure everything was in order, that the children were clean and the nursery neat.

Princess Diana pops in and out of the Highgrove and Kensington Palace nurseries all the time. Her bedroom is within listening distance of both, and her staff say that the first wail from either of the children has her out of bed and in to comfort them. Prince Charles tries to make her delegate more to the staff and stick to a happy medium in her concern for the children, but, she says, "A mother's arms are more comforting than anyone else's."

And Charles himself has broken Royal habit by often bathing the children himself. He rarely saw his father when he was a small boy. In fact, Prince Philip was more likely to write to the children than to visit the nursery.

"Papa used to send us little notes," Prince Charles once said, and indeed he did exactly the same with the two younger boys, as I knew from my own days in the nursery.

Charles, of course, adored his Nanny, Mabel Anderson, and he very much wanted her to look after his own children. A traditionalist, he would have liked her common sense and old-fashioned, solid ways to influence his own family.

Princess Diana would have none of it. She was determined to have a modern, unstarched nanny. Someone young and trained in up-to-date methods. There were a lot of tears from Mabel Anderson, who was working for Princess Anne when she was told of this decision, but the Princess was not to be moved.

So along came Nanny Barnes, who at forty-one found herself the first Royal Nanny to an heir to the throne not to have two footmen and two housemaids to do most of the boring work of bringing up babies. As it is, she just has a nursery maid, who at least does deal with the diapers.

However, Nanny Barnes, I'm told, also has her tearful

moments. British nannies are used to total authority in their nursery, and this Princess Diana will not have. She wants to be involved in every aspect of the children's upbringing.

Which may account for William's publicly recorded trail of destruction; one of his favorite pastimes is putting shoes down the john and flushing them away. In the Royal apartments anything breakable is put out of reach—including President Reagan's wedding gift of crystal.

William no doubt can get away with more with Mum than he would with his nanny, and this division of authority makes Nanny Barnes's job a difficult one.

The Queen left her children's upbringing to Mabel Anderson, but she did try to make their lives more normal than hers had been. The nursery staff called Charles, Anne, Andrew, and Edward by their Christian names. Then, when their eighteenth birthdays came along, the Lord Chamberlain sent around a note to all the staff, saying that from now on the Queen requested that her child be addressed as His or Her Royal Highness.

This is a tradition that, being titled herself, the Princess certainly approves of. But there will be no question of anyone calling the children by any nicknames. Henry might become Harry, in the English way, but William will certainly never be called Bill.

The two Royal Princes are also the first direct heirs to the throne to be born outside the Palace. Both arrived in the Lindo wing of one of London's famous hospitals.

St. Mary's, Paddington Hospital is by no means chic, but it is where Mr. George Pinker, the Royal gynecologist, operates. Mr. Pinker is also a bit of a break from tradition. He is not titled, his consulting rooms in Harley Street are at the top of a creaky old lift, he has one charming secretary called Caroline, and his consulting room is small and cozy, with just a neat desk, a comfortable chair, and pleasant pictures. There is an examination table with a small screen around it and an ordinary wooden chair to hold the patient's clothing.

Princess Diana has been known—like the rest of the young Royals—to visit this consulting room, where the gray-haired, easygoing surgeon talks straight common sense and firmly lays down the law about what he thinks is right and wrong in pregnancy.

At the Palace we were fairly sure that the Princess must be pregnant when the Royal chauffeur was instructed to take her to 96 Harley Street, and our suspicions were confirmed when Mr. Pinker appeared, trim and twinkly, at Balmoral.

It was he who insisted that the Royal babies be delivered in the hospital, refusing to have any truck with the nonsense of babies being born in what he considers the unsafe environment of the Palace.

That too caused a little flutter in the Royal dovecots. The Queen felt that tradition should be upheld and the future heir born in the Palace. Mr. Pinker would not have it, and the Princess, who trusts him implicitly, agreed. Now both babies have been born with remarkable ease at the Lindo ward.

Certainly they are both healthy children. At the time of writing, the Prince's staff haven't come to many conclusions about Prince Harry except that he seems more placid than his big brother.

The children's surroundings are also completely different from the old Royal nursery at Buckingham Palace. There, when I was Nursery Footman, I worked in a room with green walls, very simple and basic furniture, a portrait of the Queen and Prince Philip, and hardly any toys; there was a dressing-up box in the corridor outside. The only thing that made the room look like a nursery was that it had an open fireplace—which I had to keep stoking in winter. The only other room in the Palace, incidentally, to have an open fire is the Queen's sitting room.

Prince William and Prince Henry's nurseries also have an open fireplace. The Prince associates a real fire with "coziness," his favorite word. And the first thing he did at both

Highgrove and Kensington Palace was to have all the chimneys reopened.

Both the country and London nurseries are painted in soft pastel shades, unlike the hospital green of Buckingham Palace, again chosen to be "cozy." Princess Diana had the idea of having a mural of cartoon characters drawn at Highgrove, thinking it would be fun for the children. She carefully selected all the references, but when the job was finished, both she and Prince Charles were horrified. They decided it would terrify small children rather than amuse them, and Dudley Poplak, their interior decorator, was sent for with his pot of paint to cover it all over!

Though the Princess loathes horses and is not mad about dogs, it is certain that Prince Charles will have William learning to ride before he is three. And they will have to learn to care for dogs or incur their paternal grandmother's displeasure. Cats will not be a problem. Of the Royal Family, only Princess Michael of Kent likes them.

But Princess Diana will probably continue to break down many of the old Royal taboos. And at least her children are fortunate in that at present there is a rash of young Royals, plus small children from her own family. The word is that she is planning to create a little nursery school within Kensington Palace itself, something she, and William's godmother, Lady Susan Hussey, the Queen's lady-in-waiting, both have experience of running. And Lady Susan is taking an active part in plans for this project.

Prince Charles lets his wife have her head in matters to do with the children. And it seems that now with their family growing, they are settling down. Some of the earlier marital problems are going away.

All the rumors in the summer of 1982 that Princess Diana was unhappy, and that the marriage was having problems, were quite true. Everyone at the Palace was worried that the fairy-tale romance was going to collapse.

The Household were speculating privately about what on

earth could be done if it did go seriously wrong. Divorce was unthinkable. There was no question of whether Prince Charles would do his duty. But the Princess—at that time volatile, happy and unhappy by turns, imperious and then pathetic—was the unknown quantity. Everyone was nervous about what she might do.

The feeling among the public in Britain was that the Princess had made a terrible mistake and could not stand the pressure of being Royal. It was pointed out that she was not a "stayer." She had never seen anything through: schools, jobs, training, even dancing classes were abandoned before the finish. Was she going to abandon being Royal?

The answer, of course, was no. Friends in the Palace were telling me that it was not the Princess who had doubts; it was the Prince. And I was not at all surprised. He was concerned that he might have married someone who could not cope with "the job," as he calls it, but he was also experiencing a disruption of his entire life. All those who had been closest to him were melting away into other jobs. He was finding his freedom to choose his own friends and pastimes curtailed. For the first time he had to consider someone other than himself.

He had, as I knew well, been the bachelor par excellence, tumbling in and out of love but with an unerring instinct for picking discreet companions. His two detectives, Paul Officer and John McClean, and I—though not exactly his friends —would have done anything for him, and felt enormous affection for him. Paul Officer, who once saved the Prince's life, left on the day of the wedding. By the summer of '82 I had gone, and John McClean was talking of leaving. And has indeed now left.

The Princess was not well disposed to people who had been part of his previous life. Though we did resent it to some extent, in retrospect her attitude was normal. She wanted the Prince to be all hers—fresh, clean, and shiny, with the past finished and done. Not surprising for a nineteen-year-old girl in love and with no experience of her own. We were reminders of different days.

Also, our jobs had completely changed now that he had a wife. The policemen were back to being guardians rather than companions. Many of my tasks—looking after his clothes, seeing he was properly dressed, laying out the right tie, and arranging his meals—were the kind of small things that I did because I was paid to but which a young bride would want to do out of love. The job as I knew it had ended, and so I decided to resign.

The Prince was miserable seeing change all about him, and the Princess was being difficult and throwing the odd tantrum, determined to have her way. Palace inside information believes that the turning point came when they had a flaming row on the night of the Remembrance Festival at the Royal Albert Hall. The Royal Family arrived, as they arrive every November, but without Princess Diana. She wasn't well, the Prince said, and made her excuses.

Astonishingly, she suddenly appeared, after the Queen—considered very bad form—and breathless. She had capitulated from whatever position she had taken, and after that things calmed down.

As Lady Diana, the Princess had no doubts at all about what she had chosen. She went after the Prince with single-minded determination. She wanted him, and she got him. She still wants him, but it had to be on his terms, as it was all through the engagement, and that gradually happened.

She went through a difficult pregnancy, which didn't help. She was unable to join him when he went out hunting, which she resented; that caused problems. She did manage to continue to cope with personal chores for him, but when ordering his meals from Mervyn, the chef, she would say, "My usual, please." Her usual was bacon and tomatoes. She ate nothing else for many weeks.

So there was a sticky period while a lot of adjusting went on.

Many of her original "musts" are disappearing. At first, freedom was the cry. Particularly the freedom to go off to the hairdresser when she liked, just as she had done when she was living in her own flat with her girlfriends. I think the Princess has now realized that freedom is another ten minutes in the bath and then having the hairdresser come to her place—not she to his place.

She is superb with the public, has learned every Royal knack, and always looks wonderful, particularly in the evenings. As buying clothes was always a favorite pastime, she has every opportunity to indulge herself with this pleasure.

She is changing and growing up all the time. During the Royal tours last year to Australia and Canada, which were considered a triumph by all, her genuine warmth and liking for people were evident. Prince Charles used to say to those who accompanied them on the tour, "I might just as well stay in the car. They've all come to see her."

Her style has changed too. She has become a fashion leader, wearing hats all the time. I never saw a hat in sight during the engagement. And she has revived the Queen Alexandra choker fashion. I remember when she first came to the Palace, the Prince gave her a beautiful pendant made of diamonds and emeralds in the Prince of Wales feathers. It came from the safe downstairs: a family heirloom left by Queen Mary.

It was one of his first gifts to her, and she always wore it on a velvet ribbon that matched whichever dress she was wearing. Today she wears it on a necklace of diamonds, part of the £600,000 wedding present from Saudi Arabia. I can confirm the figure, as we had it valued immediately. For insurance purposes, of course.

The velvet ribbon is gone forever.

Unlike the other Royal ladies—and as the youngest of the Spencer girls—she had hardly any jewelry when she arrived at the Palace. She owned a signet ring with the letter *D* on it, and that was about it.

For her engagement photographs, *Vogue* magazine lent her the green dress, and she borrowed jewelry from Collingwood, who wanted to present her with the jewels because she admired them so much. But the Palace advisers said no. Since she was to become Royalty, the rule of "no commercial acceptance of goods" applied. Not surprisingly, the Princess's face fell. "I'm not a Royal yet," she protested.

Collingwood's kind thought was not forgotten. They still have her patronage—unlike Garrard, who supplied her sapphire-and-diamond engagement ring. The Prince was convinced that the jeweler leaked the story of the tray of rings that was sent to Windsor for the Princess to choose from. They knew an engagement must be imminent, and talked. Prince Charles was furious, and sent for Mr. Summer, the director at Garrard, to give him the Royal heave-ho. It was a brief visit; I showed him in and I showed him out in what seemed no time at all.

It's strange, really: the Royal Family always look to the staff for leaks when they are trying to keep secrets. But nine times out of ten the information comes from much higher up.

The biggest leak I witnessed was the engagement. William Rees-Mogg, then editor of *The Times*, had published the scoop of the century in a small box, halfway down the front page. The news had been leaked to him, off the record, by his old friend Edward Heath, the ex–Prime Minister. In Britain, those who have been Prime Minister remain lifetime members of the Privy Council. If a Royal is marrying, the Privy Council has to be informed. Most people could not believe that Heath would be so indiscreet, but Prince Charles was convinced that he was the source. The Prince was furious, but resigned himself to the situation. Altogether, both he and the Princess were cross with a number of people once the wedding was over.

He said to me, after the honeymoon, when we were back at the Palace, "I can't believe Lord Lichfield could have let us down so badly." Lord Lichfield, the Queen's cousin, had been commissioned to take the wedding pictures. He had taken a spontaneous, marvelous shot of the entire wedding group, collapsed and giggling. He must have made a fortune with this one picture. It was reproduced literally everywhere. "He never even submitted the pictures to the Queen," Prince Charles grumbled.

It was more a grumble than a rage. Lord Lichfield is sort of "family," and the Royals don't get so upset if relatives make money out of them. They aren't so keen on anyone else doing so, though.

The Prince and Princess were both angry with the Emmanuels, the couple who made the wedding dress. They felt the designers got far too much personal publicity out of it. So the Emmanuels are definitely *out*.

In an effort to get back in again, the Emmanuels sent a beautiful photograph album in white leather with "The Dress" tooled in gold on the cover. The Princess saw this for the first time in Scotland, on the second part of the honeymoon. It was a pictorial record of the highly secret making of her wedding dress, including photographs of the press jostling outside their premises, the Emmanuels themselves having a day off from the pressures, and finishing with a photograph of the dress itself in all its creaseable glory.

"Just look at this," the Princess said to me, flipping through the pages. "How can I get these silly pictures out and use the book for something else?"

I had no suggestions, but thought privately that she was rapidly becoming a real Royal.

One person might have been justly cross with them—the Aga Khan. They completely forgot to invite him to the wedding, and had the Queen not met him at a race meeting, he might never have received his invitation. He did not fit into conventional Royalty, or any other category, when the lists were made up by the Lord Chamberlain's office.

"See you at the wedding in July, then," the Queen had

told him as they parted. Rather embarrassed, the Aga Khan informed her that he had not been invited. It was, of course, quickly put right, but how the horse-mad Royals could have forgotten anyone to do with racing and breeding beats me!

The Princess doesn't care for horses, and I must say I feel for her, having had twelve years of trying to become accustomed to them myself. The Prince tries to involve everyone around him in his favorite sport, like it or not. He used to take me to polo and foxhunting. The Princess has changed a lot of things about the Prince, but I think she will never manage to eradicate his love of anything equestrian.

She has changed his lifestyle a little. I noticed he was wearing a yellow pullover for the Prince William picture session. The times I'd tried to get him to wear yellow! My favorite color—yet I knew he would have had a fit if I'd bought anything in it, and back it would have gone.

More serious, from a family point of view, is that he has given up shooting. The Princess doesn't like that sport, perhaps because there was a great to-do at Balmoral about her supposedly shooting and not cleanly killing a stag. It was all nonsense, of course, and never happened, but it caused a terrible fuss in the press and upset the Prince. He spent a day on the phone haranguing his press secretary to try to make newspapers retract the story.

The Prince's guns are particularly fine. Made by the famous gunsmith Purdey, they belonged to King George VI. When I worked for him, they were insured for £20,000.

The Prince has now given his guns to Prince Andrew. The game staff in Norfolk and Scotland are agitated, since they must look to him for their future. Prince Edward isn't at all sporty, and Prince Andrew only plays at it. Neither of them is a truly country person. Prince Andrew's idea of a good weekend is to be at the Palace entertaining girls like Koo Stark or dancers from the Royal Ballet while the Queen is at Windsor.

What worries the country staff is that if Prince Philip gives up too as he gets older, who will lead the shoot? When Royalty likes a sport, it becomes popular. Polo has taken on a new lease of life because the Prince plays. Carriage-driving has taken off in Britain because of Prince Philip's interest. With shooting, it's not just the sport but the backup. Game-keepers worry about their future; the dog trainers, the breeders, the loaders, and the beaters worry. The Queen did indeed say, when she heard that the Prince had given his guns to Andrew, "He had better take shooting seriously again if he wants to stay a member of this family."

I remember once, when we were out shooting, the Prince shot a grouse—but it got its own back. It was coming for us like a rocket, with the wind behind it.

"Duck!" he shouted. We both ducked, while the Prince held his gun in front of his face. The grouse hit the butt of the gun and broke the stock clean in half. Happily the Prince was unhurt. We sent the gun back to Purdey to be mended, with the insurance paying.

Mind you, it is not the first time the Prince has given up shooting. I remember once, years ago, he came under the influence of a girl called Zoë Sallas. She was something of a mystery girlfriend, who turned up in 1979. For her he not only gave up shooting and fishing but turned vegetarian too —much to the irritation of the chef, who soon ran out of egg ideas. All this ended when the romance died.

It is a little strange that the Princess likes neither hunting, shooting, nor fishing—the three "musts" for the country rich in Britain—particularly as she was brought up in the countryside in a grand manner. The Spencer family live in considerable style. They have been associated with Althorp (pronounced "Althrop"), their country seat in Northamptonshire, for generations.

Nor is friendship with Royalty anything unusual in their family. A John Spencer was knighted by Henry VIII. Sir Robert, the second Spencer to be knighted, was created the first Baron Spencer by Queen Elizabeth I. He owned 19,000 sheep, and was said to be the richest man in England then. His grandson was made Earl of Sunderland by Charles I. And the grandson's son was chief adviser to Charles II, James II, and also William III.

The Spencers became truly rich when the Earl of Sunderland's son married Lady Anne Churchill, daughter of the first Duke of Marlborough and an ancestor of Winston, the most famous Churchill of them all. It was this wealth, which the Spencer family inherited from the Churchills, that gave them the opportunity to indulge their taste for the art treasures that still enrich Althorp even today.

From her birth Lady Diana was surrounded by people accustomed to the idea of close relationships with their Sovereign and a tradition of service to the Monarchy. Her father was Equerry to George VI and the present Queen; her maternal grandmother, Lady Fermoy, is the Queen Mother's closest friend. Her sister Jane is married to Mr. Robert Fellowes, the Queen's Assistant Private Secretary and son of Sir William Fellowes, who was the Queen's land agent at Sandringham.

Althorp is a fine house, far grander than many other stately homes, and certainly grander than the Queen's Norfolk home, Sandringham House. Sandringham was bought in 1862 for the astonishing amount of £220,000. It is one of the largest private homes in England, furnished with a mishmash of bad taste. But even so, it is a comfortable home with a warm and friendly atmosphere. There is one beautiful room, the main drawing room, used by the Royals for Royal teas. It is white and gilt, decorated by Queen Alexandra, and contains a priceless collection of Fabergé. But even central heating did not arrive at Sandringham until 1977.

Althorp, on the other hand, is what you might call regal. The original house was built by Sir John Spencer in the early sixteenth century. Made of red brick, it was surrounded by a moat, but since then many alterations have been made to the rooms. In 1786 the moat was filled in and the gardens and the park improved.

Today Althorp houses one of the finest art collections in Europe, with many paintings by Gainsborough and Reynolds. There are marble figures, rescued from the River Tiber in Rome, as well as treasures that once belonged to the unfortunate Queen Marie Antoinette of France. A comfortable sitting room's walls are lined with Rubenses. There are State bedrooms and ballrooms. It is a grand and magnificent house. The picture gallery is one hundred fifteen feet long, and is lined with portraits of each generation of the family since the time of Elizabeth I. As in Elizabethan times, this gallery is still used as a promenade on wet days, and is also the setting for presentations and banquets.

The house is huge, and has given a roof to many Monarchs during its history. It became the home of the future Queen of England in 1975, when her grandfather died and her father became the eighth Earl.

Countess Spencer, the Princess's stepmother, does have good taste and fine style. She has done a great deal to improve the house. But she is not a popular woman in Britain, mainly because of her high-handed, grand behavior. The British feel she is a little over the top for the middle-class-born daughter of Barbara Cartland, the highly successful romance writer.

The public also find her progression confusing: she was Raine McCorquodale; who then became The Honorable Mrs. Gerald Legge; she then became Viscountess Lewisham; followed rapidly by a new title, Countess of Dartmouth, on the death of her husband's father. Then this rather forceful lady, who once caused a scene at a London airport over dirty teacups, upped and divorced the Earl of Dartmouth to marry yet another Earl, the Princess's father.

I must say I rather liked her. She calls everybody "darling," even the butler. She adores being a countess and relishes her grand surroundings. And why not?

THE WALES FAMILY

But her heart must have plummeted when she came to the Palace on the eve of the engagement. I had to usher her and Earl Spencer into the Prince's simple set of rooms overlooking the Mall for a so-called celebration. As none of them drank, I could see her looking around for something complimentary to say about the surroundings. She settled for silence. With a flash of inspiration, she did manage to compliment me about the "clever" elevator on the way out.

I suppose it was understandable that she would have expected grander surroundings for the future King of England. The Prince's rooms were decorated in a slightly modern style in 1969 by his cousin by marriage, designer David Hicks. David Hicks chose all the furniture from spares within the Palace—nothing new was bought. It is, honestly, all rather ordinary, basically Victorian, in mahogany. The only outstanding feature was a huge four-poster, which the Prince has now had moved to his new home at Kensington Palace. The bedroom walls were painted green, the sitting room was painted blue, and later he designed his own study, which is mostly dark brown.

Comfortable rather than grand, as it was, the Prince was always very happy in his apartment. His tastes are simple. Highgrove, his country home in Gloucestershire, is much less formal than the house that was the Princess's home after her father came into the title. But she spent little time at Althorp after her father married the present Countess in 1976. He bought her the flat in Coleherne Court in the Earls Court area of London, where I used to collect her in those early, exciting days of the Prince's courtship. She rarely went home to Northampton.

There is a coolness between the Earl's wife and his four children, who are Diana, her sisters Jane and Sarah, and the heir, Charles. You can sense it when they are all together; everyone is a fraction too polite. What must irritate the children enormously when they do go home is a particular portrait of their stepmother. The Countess has a chocolate-box type of beauty, and there is a vast, chocolate-box painting of her on the staircase of the house, mixed in with the marvelous collection of Reynoldses and Gainsboroughs. The portrait is desperately out of place. I don't doubt that, when the house passes on to the Earl's children, it will be the first thing to go.

So, one way and another, it didn't seem likely that the Princess would be intimidated by Buckingham Palace when she moved in for the waiting time between her engagement to Prince Charles and the day of the wedding. Yet, in a strange way, she wasn't comfortable there.

She seemed uncertain of exactly how to play her role; she was so friendly that I was constantly uneasy she would be too informal with the staff. There are divisions that both staff and Royals have to learn and observe instinctively. There isn't a book of rules handed out with either job. I was afraid her warmth and chattiness might make some of those in Royal service take advantage. In fact, I did tick off one of the footmen for being too familiar with her.

The Prince was always asking me to keep an eye on his fiancée. His last words every morning were, "Look after Lady Diana," while his first inquiry when he came home was, "How's Lady Diana? Is she all right?" He worried about her being lonely. Particularly when he went on a Royal tour to Australia just after the engagement, and I went with him. The staff said she became a little like a Princess in the Tower at that time, though she went shopping and buzzed about in her own car. For all her determination to keep her freedom, I think, in retrospect, even that early it was beginning to dawn on her that she would never really be free again. She had her first example of this the morning after the engagement. She asked me, "Where's my car?"

"It's down in the quadrangle," I told her, "where you left it last night."

"Oh, good," she said. "I'm just going out for a while."

I took her downstairs, since she wasn't that familiar with

the Palace yet, and walked her out to where her red Metro was parked. As she climbed into the driver's seat, the door on the other side opened, and Paul Officer, one of the Prince's policemen, joined her.

"It's all right," she said. "I can manage."

"Sorry—we're part of your life now," he told her.

It was a situation she found restricting. Not long after that, she made her first staff change: she found Paul too set in the Prince's ways for her liking, and too protective and fatherly towards her. She didn't like it—as I suppose any other nineteen-year-old wouldn't like it. Paul gave in his notice. Since she was going to become Royal, one of the rules she had to learn was how the division between staff and Royalty operates. And in the end, the lesson that sank in was given by one of the pantry staff.

I was constantly hearing that she had been down to the kitchen or one of the various pantries for a chat. She'd come away with an apple or some yogurt. I tried tactfully to stop these visits by seeing that the fridge in her own apartment was always stocked up with things she liked. She had three rooms: a bedroom, a sitting room, and a small kitchen. It was the apartment in which Miss Peebles, the governess to all the Royal children, had lived for many years. The Prince himself had supervised the creation of the rooms into a charming little retreat. But while he was away, Lady Diana seemed to need to roam the corridors, and the kitchens were a favorite stopping place.

Some of the older Staff at the Palace resented this. Others, of course, thought it was smashing to see her. But the kitchen staff are hardworking folk, and when something goes wrong—as it often does in a busy kitchen—they let rip. The air can be blue. At those times they weren't too keen on turning around to find the future Princess of Wales standing behind them, tall, doe-eyed, innocent, and shy, asking, Could she have an apple, please?

At first one of the yeomen used to encourage her to gossip

with him and promptly passed on what she had said. Then there was a staff change. The Yeoman of the Glass and China took over. One day the Princess came tripping in when the Court was at Sandringham, and the Staff were particularly pressed. The Yeoman said to her bluntly, stabbing a finger at the door, "Through there is your side of the house, Your Royal Highness, and through here is my side of the house."

She blushed scarlet, fled, and never went back to the kitchens again.

Prince Charles was right to be anxious about her. She was desperately lonely in the early days. There were times when she simply didn't know what to do with herself, which isn't exactly surprising when one remembers just how young she was. She continued her walkabouts in the Palace corridors, but now with a Sony Walkman clamped over her ears for company.

That in itself wasn't in character. She doesn't like a lot of noise. I was amused when I saw she had taken earplugs to a Rolling Stones concert. I remember the earplugs well; she had sent out for them one day at Sandringham after the Staff and I had thrown a late-night party, forgetting we were above her rooms.

The Prince, who could sleep through a hurricane, hadn't heard us, but she had. But the Prince was crotchety too, because the Princess had made them change their rooms. I felt very guilty at the time for forgetting that Sandringham is a lot smaller than either Althorp or Buckingham Palace, and noise is therefore more easily heard.

Their own house, Highgrove, is small by Royal standards, too, and quite simple. I remember the Prince coming back to his rooms at Buckingham Palace, highly amused, after seeing his mother.

"Do you know what the Queen said to me?" he asked. He had a habit of prefacing information with a question.

"No, sir," I said dutifully.

"She asked me the name of the house I was buying. When

I said Highgrove, she said it sounded like something in Wimbledon.''

Well, Wimbledon is a middle-class London suburb; Highgrove is not. But the house isn't vast. It is neither old nor architecturally interesting. It is just a pleasant English country house with several cottages in the grounds of some three hundred acres. That is such a small amount of land, by Royal standards, that Princess Diana goes to Badminton Park when she wants a long walk. But Highgrove suits the Prince admirably. He bought it—or, rather, the Duchy of Cornwall, from which he gets his income, did. The administrators of the Duchy had been looking for something suitable and came up with Highgrove in Gloucestershire.

The house was built around two hundred years ago in the Georgian, rather severe style and is just about the right size for the Prince until his family grows some more. The entrance hall is impressive, very wide, running from one end of the house to the other. The floor is highly polished and covered with Oriental rugs. A fine staircase goes off to the right. When the Prince bought the house, this was painted white. He personally began stripping it back to the wood. The builders finished the job.

Downstairs there are four rooms. The Princess's sitting room is in sunny yellow, the only room in this color. Next door is the formal drawing room, with pictures borrowed from the Queen's collection on the greeny-whitewashed walls. On the other side is the Prince's study, painted in a beigy color—the room is too small to take dark colors. And finally, there is the dining room, which seats sixteen, but is rarely used. They prefer to eat in front of the television in Princess Diana's sitting room. Upstairs are four suites—and a small nursery for the Royal babies.

I went down to see it with him just after the Duchy had completed the sale.

"What do you think?" he asked, as anxious as anyone about his first home purchase.

I said I could see why it appealed to him. The house is easy to reach from the Buckingham Palace side of London. Also, at that time, it had another advantage. It is in the countryside where the Beaufort Hunt meets, making his near neighbors Camilla Parker Bowles and her husband. It is also within easy driving distance of his sister, Princess Anne, and her husband, Captain Mark Phillips, at their home, Gatcombe Park.

One of his reasons for buying the house is no longer valid. He does not see the Parker Bowleses anymore. They are a little old for the Princess, and she resented stories suggesting that Camilla had been a great influence on the Prince in his bachelor days.

The Prince, the policeman on duty, and I used to go to work on the house every weekend. But Highgrove was nowhere near ready when he married, because he had hung back from buying too many things. He had the whole place painted white and left it at that.

"I'm bound to get lots of things when I marry," he used to say. So the house was rather quaintly furnished with some new bits and pieces—chiefly new beds—which I bought, and anything suitable dug out from the Royal storerooms. Mostly gifts received on Royal tours.

Indeed, he did get a lot of gifts when he married: a treasure house full. There was a positive surplus of kitchens. The Royal couple were given so many splendid kitchens by manufacturers that they could choose the two best for Highgrove and Kensington Palace. The rest were installed in the estate cottages, raising their value no end.

We were keeping very quiet about all this, until one of the manufacturers broke the rules by saying *their* kitchen was at Highgrove. It was not, and there were red faces—including Royal ones—when we had to say that no, their kitchen was not in the house. Actually, a German kitchen was chosen, as it was the best of the lot.

Not many people get a swimming pool as a wedding present. The Prince and Princess did—a fine gift bought with a collection taken up by the workers on the bride's father's estate. The army dug the hole. As far as I know, Her Majesty's navy didn't put the water in.

But of course the Waleses (as they are known) spend more time in London, living at Kensington Palace, where they have two apartments that have been knocked into one. Numbers eight and nine.

Kensington Palace, a complex of old houses and a small palace set at the side of Kensington Gardens, is used by the Royals but maintained by the Department of the Environment. It is full of grace-and-favor residences. Bennett, the Queen's retired Back Stairs Page, has an apartment there. So do Prince and Princess Michael of Kent. The Duke and Duchess of Gloucester have a charming small house, next to Princess Margaret.

The Waleses' section includes a morning room, which is used as a waiting room for those coming for an audience with the Prince. There is a private and formal dining room on the first floor, the big kitchen, and a drawing room that will hold sixty people in what would have been the second apartment.

Also on the first floor are the bedroom and a dressing room for the Princess. The Prince and Princess sleep in the huge four-poster bed that he took with him from his rooms at the Palace.

Above them on the second floor are Prince William and Prince Henry's nursery, along with two guest bedrooms, which usually house ladies-in-waiting. Over the kitchen and dining room are three Staff rooms.

Prince Charles had planned to have his offices in his apartments. But in the end he decided to keep them at the Palace, as the printing presses, post office, and press room are there, and he is left with more space in his home.

Curiously, the rooms at Kensington Palace have ended up looking just like those at Highgrove. Dudley Poplak, decorator to the Princess's mother, Mrs. Shand Kydd, did both homes. The Princess followed her mother's influence in choosing pinks and beiges, which are also her own favorite colors.

The pinks and beiges do give a soft, cozy look, rather than the grand style affected by the Princess's London neighbor, Princess Michael of Kent. I was asked what color I should like my rooms, and I'm afraid I stuck to my favorite yellow.

The apartment is charming, but by no means grand. Should anything happen to the Queen Mother, it is possible that the Prince and Princess would take over her home, Clarence House. This house in the Mall is where the Queen lived when she was heir to the throne.

"But I don't think I'd want it," Prince Charles used to say. "Far too expensive to run."

His present household is run by a butler. Prince Charles will not be eligible for a page or even a sergeant-footman until he is King. That recalls when the late King, discovering that the Lord Mayor of London had created the post of Sergeant-Footman for his office, thundered: "There is only one Sergeant Footman and he is mine."

As far as the Waleses are concerned, this means that their household arrangements are more like those of ordinary rich people. For the time being.

The butler Alan Fisher is a man in his early fifties, who has also been butler to the Duke of Windsor in Paris, and Bing Crosby in Hollywood. His great ambition after Bing Crosby died was to work for the Prince. While working for the millionaire Whitneys in New York, he wrote three times to the Palace applying for the job. He is an absolutely brilliant butler, and was most put out to be told by the Prince's secretary that there was no vacancy.

His luck changed one weekend when we went to stay with the Spencers. It was the first time the Princess had been back to the house since her wedding. The Countess was giving an enormous party for the estate, at which the workers were

THE WALES FAMILY

going to present their wedding gift, funds towards the High-grove swimming pool.

The staff were in a bit of a panic at the idea of a Royal visit. With her usual style, the Countess flew Alan over from New York for the weekend to run the whole show. I had met him several times before, as the Royal servant world is a small one. I was delighted to see a friendly face, and highly amused at the Countess, who constantly called him "Alan darling." The mind boggles at the thought of a Royal using the same terms of endearment.

It was the first time the Princess of Wales had met him, and she was impressed. She and the Prince went out for a walk on Sunday morning, and she had obviously made up her mind that Alan was the butler for her. When they got back to Althorp, Alan and I met them at the front door. As they were taking their coats off, Prince Charles asked him, "When you leave here, what will you do?"

"I suppose I shall go back to New York and stay with my present family, sir," Alan said.

The Prince said, in his rather diffident way, "I suppose you wouldn't come and work for me?"

There was a silence, and then Alan told him, "Well, sir, I have written to you three times, only to be told no."

"What?" Prince Charles said. "I knew nothing about it."

"Well, that's how it is, sir," Alan said, adding smartly that he would love to come and work for him.

Michael Colborne had to do a lot of back-pedaling when Alan arrived at the Prince's invitation. That was no bad thing for staff, as it put them in a stronger position.

It was splendid while it lasted, but eventually he and the Princess did not get on. No one could work out what he did, but he obviously upset her and she hardly spoke to him. Prince Charles gave all the orders and kept the peace. So many employees had left him since his marriage that he must have been getting anxious about his image. And apart from anything else, he hates constant change, trouble, and chill atmosphere. Nevertheless, Alan handed in his notice. I suspect he found the job not quite what he had expected. He was used by the Waleses for everything *except* the traditional butler's duties after he arrived at Kensington Palace.

It's unusual for the Prince to give a big dinner party, as it would be difficult to get two dozen friends together. For instance, his old friends, like the Tryons and the Parker Bowleses, are not popular with the Princess. Lady Sarah Keswick, daughter of Lord Dalhousie, the Queen Mother's Chamberlain, doesn't like Prince Charles's greatest friends, the Van Cutsems, and avoids being at the same table with them. Making up the guest list for a dinner combining friends of the Prince's age—the older people he prefers—with those of the Princess's age group is difficult.

One day I caught Alan in a very bad temper indeed. He was, he said, doing everything except looking after the dining room: answering the door, tidying desks, even doing a bit of redecorating, and generally running about.

"I've had enough," he told me. "I said to the Prince, 'Just call me when you have invited twenty-four for dinner, and I'll do it for you gladly.' "

"You didn't!" I said.

"Oh yes, I did," he said crossly.

Life for everyone will become more pleasant when the Waleses have the time and opportunity to get their own "set" together. What with the Princess's two pregnancies and the overseas tours they have undertaken, there hasn't been much chance to create a social life.

And the Princess is still not as certain of herself as she seems on public occasions. In private, there is a lot of anxiety, and her lack of confidence makes her difficult to work for. If she gets the slightest hint of feeling that someone is not 110% on her side, she becomes suspicious and difficult. Her Private Secretary, Oliver Everett, was hanging in there by a hair's breadth when I left. He has now been made the Deputy Librarian at Windsor. She has even fallen out with Evelyn, her dresser, who came on the honeymoon with us.

It is a shame, because she and Evelyn got on so well, but now there is another favorite dresser, Valerie. Valerie was a housekeeper, but as the Waleses don't need one, it was decided that the Princess would have two dressers. Valerie is now Number One; there were tears from Evelyn when it was suddenly decided that the ex-housekeeper should go on the Australian tour instead of Evelyn. She probably no longer cares, since she is marrying the Prince's chauffeur.

Still, it must have given a small glow of satisfaction when a frantic S.O.S. came from New Zealand for six more hats, as the Princess hadn't taken enough. They went off by air in the diplomatic bag. It seemed a lot of bother, as the tour was nearly over, but Royals don't like being photographed in the same hat twice. For a girl who never wore them, the Princess must now have as many hats as the Queen Mother.

I suppose I left Royal service through the same falling from grace, to some extent. The Princess barely spoke to me for weeks. When I left, she didn't say goodbye. But then, when I met her in the street one day, coming out of Turnbull & Asser, where she had been to choose some shirts for the Prince, she couldn't have been nicer.

As I passed the shop door, I heard a familiar voice say, "Good afternoon, Stephen." I was amazed to see it was the Princess, wearing the white coat she'd worn on her honeymoon. I automatically bowed.

"Oh, don't be silly!" she said. "How are you?"

"I'm very well," I told her.

"Are you surviving outside?"

"Oh, yes," I said. "I'm just off to America on tour."

She nodded. "We're off on our own tour to Australia. But it won't be too bad, because we're taking William with us."

A small crowd had started to gather, and her detective, Alan Peters, began to look nervous. I thought perhaps I ought to extricate both of us. "Please give my best wishes to the Prince," I said.

"I promise," she said, and got into her car.

Later that evening I rang Alan Fisher, and said I'd bumped into her shopping.

"I don't want her to think I was lying in wait," I told him.

"No, don't worry," he said. "She came back very amused at seeing you."

When I heard that the Prince had given up shooting, the thought did cross my mind that maybe this would not be much of a hardship for him. He is such a kind and basically gentle person that all the killing that his father so enjoys is a bit out of character.

And his tastes outside of sport are rather highbrow—classical music, opera, and the like. Opera is the great love, and fortunately I am mad about it too. I was lucky enough to go often to the Royal Opera House, accompanying him to the Royal Box, something that most opera buffs would give their eyeteeth for.

A measure of his kindness I remember well was the night that we took the late Princess Alice, Countess of Athlone (his great-aunt), with us. The Princess, who was extremely deaf, had a clever hearing gadget on the ends of her glasses, so she used her spectacles for both seeing and hearing. We were nicely settled in the Royal Box along with Squadron Leader Checketts, the Prince's Private Secretary at the time, who was making up the party. The curtain had just gone up, when there was a distressed cry from Princess Alice.

"My glasses!" she called. "I've dropped my glasses."

Like most deaf people, without her hearing aid she was inclined to shout. The cry of "My glasses!" reverberated around the Opera House.

"Don't worry, Aunt Alice," the Prince whispered. "I'll find them for you."

"They're down there, somewhere," she bellowed.

"Don't worry, don't worry," he kept saying, trying to

THE WALES FAMILY

whisper and get through to her at the same time. The three of us went down on our hands and knees, scrabbling in the dark.

"Charles—I can't hear anything," she complained loudly from above.

We could hear her, and so could half the audience, if not the cast. It was a great relief when David Checketts retrieved her glasses from under her seat.

"Sorry about that," the Prince said to us afterwards. "Thanks for helping."

He is considerate. I remember another pre-Diana occasion when he, John McClean, and I were driving through Glasgow on our way to Holyrood House, another Royal stopping-off place, this one being in Edinburgh. It once housed the tragic—or traitorous, whichever way you look at it— Mary, Queen of Scots. The Royals stay there for a week every July as an official visit to Scotland.

John—also no longer in the Prince's employ—was driving, and the Prince suddenly said, as we came to an area known as the Gorbals, "John, doesn't your mother live here?"

"That's right, sir," said John.

"Would you like to stop and see her?" the Prince asked.

The Gorbals is one of the toughest spots in Britain.

"I don't think so, sir," John said, poker-faced. "She'll be out mugging people right now."

He must miss John a lot. John McClean, a marvelous sportsman and great companion, had been with him for fourteen years. And he could *nearly* get away with murder with Prince Charles, but he knew just how far he could go with a touch of *lèse-majesté*.

Abroad, and often in the country, John would actually join the dinner party as a guest. If something about the host or hostess or one of the guests annoyed the Prince—Royal manners forbade his stating so—he would use John as his mouthpiece. Before the evening began, he would tell John exactly what his feelings were. For John, a nod was as good as a wink and, taking the hint, he would voice the Prince's opinions.

After the meal the Prince would say, "I'm so sorry. I can't control McClean."

The Prince always liked to drive for the first twenty or so miles when we were going anywhere, and then he'd hand the wheel over to John and have a quiet nap. He can catnap any time, any place. One evening, John had had a couple of drinks and was feeling mischievous. As we were driving through a small village, he began to wave to the people, copying the Prince's Royal style.

Something woke the Prince, who stared at John suspiciously, and said, "What are you doing?"

"Just waving for you while you were asleep, sir," John said cheekily.

We very often drove ourselves, but some official occasions required a chauffeur and a Rolls-Royce. The Prince had an engagement at Eastbourne, on the south coast of England, one day. We went off with Paul Officer as his detective (the one who left on the day of the wedding) and David Check-etts. We had an unfamiliar chauffeur driving us, one of the ten who are employed in the Royal Mews.

All was well until we started to drive back to Windsor, a distance of about a hundred miles, all across country. I don't know whether the chauffeur had it in mind to cut down the time driving back, or if he'd had a few drinks while he was waiting, but he drove like a lunatic.

Paul Officer, as a police superintendent, more or less commanded him to slow down, but he wouldn't. We were all being thrown about, bounced over railway crossings, and the Prince and David Checketts, both of whom had been sitting in the back, swore they were black-and-blue when we got back to Windsor. I've never seen the Prince so angry.

THE WALES FAMILY

Next morning he rang Sir John Miller and said he never wanted that chauffeur to drive him again. It was an unusual thing for him to do. He is normally very gentle about staff.

The man wasn't fired; he was demoted. But we never saw him again. And he'd given us something to talk about for a day or two.

Paul Officer, who was with us that day, had also been with the Prince for many years. He came into the Royalty Protection Service a year after John. Twice he saved the Prince's life, once when the Prince suffered from heatstroke in Palm Beach, Florida, after a polo match—a story I told in *Royal Service*.

Even more dramatic was the time that the Prince was in the navy at Portland Naval Base. They were in shore barracks, Paul in the room next door to the Prince's. Suddenly he was awakened in the early hours of the morning by a crashing noise coming from the Prince's room.

Knowing the Prince should have been alone, he rushed next door immediately, to find a fellow naval officer in the room, demented, and trying to attack the Prince with a chair. The Prince, being in bed, was at a terrible disadvantage. Paul managed to pull the man away and then, with the Prince's help, to overpower him.

At the time we were all sworn to secrecy, but of course inevitably the story broke. But what no one discovered was that several months later, when the Prince joined his next ship, he was horrified to find that one of his fellow officers was the very same man who had attacked him. He was angry at such a breach of security, and so was Paul Officer. They could hardly believe that such a potentially dangerous situation could have been permitted to happen.

But when I look back, the Prince's bachelor days were on the whole pretty good, and it's not surprising he was in no hurry to marry, in spite of his father's nagging and his mother's anxiety. He had his own companions, admittedly—but we all got on well and had a great deal of fun, both in far-flung places and nearer home.

One of the secret Royal hideaways is a tiny house called Tamarisk on the Scilly Isles, off the coast of Cornwall. We'd sometimes go there for the weekend—the Prince, John McClean, usually Checketts, and myself. Tamarisk is a comfortable house, furnished in an ordinary style, just like anybody's simple holiday home. It's in the loveliest spot in the world. When Prince William and Prince Henry are a little older, they're bound to be taken off there for summer sea-and-sand holidays.

Set back from the ocean and not overlooked by anyone, the house has two main bedrooms, two bathrooms (one off the main bedroom), servants' rooms in an attic conversion, and curly staircases. There's a sitting room, a dining room off the kitchen, and a pretty garden. It's run by a nice lady called Mrs. Hall. The Prince and Princess used it as a quiet getaway place on their honeymoon, and the Princess adored it.

All sorts of people use Tamarisk, which, because it belongs to the Duchy of Cornwall and the Duchy belongs to the Prince, means it is his house. But the Kents love it and go there often. So do people from the Prince's Household, and so does Bennett, the Queen's retired Page of the Back Stairs. He was always asking me if I would mind asking the Prince if he could go there, please.

I remember one weekend we'd been out on a fishing boat all day long, spinning for mackerel. We had caught an awful lot. So we had a great divide-up among us. John McClean brought back bags of them, and they stank out the back of the plane.

The evening after the big fishing, the Duchy provided us with lobster for supper, which Mrs. Hall prepared beautifully. After dinner we switched on the TV and were watching *Hamlet* starring Lord Olivier. It was a bit heavy going, and the Prince fell sound asleep in his chair. Checketts's lobster couldn't have been quite right, because he spent most of the evening excusing himself, saying he was doing some work, but in such a small house we knew perfectly well he was in the bathroom, being ill, poor man.

With Checketts in and out, the Prince sound asleep, and Lord Olivier doing his "To be, or not to be," John McClean and I were desperately bored, but we didn't dare change the program because it wasn't our TV.

When the Prince woke up, he found the thought of Checketts throwing up all evening hilariously funny. The Royals do, I'm afraid, have a habit of enjoying other people's discomfiture.

Checketts, of course, was Household and could get a bit grand on occasions. He was jealous of his position with the Prince, and that was what led to his leaving in the end. He was becoming too bossy and too possessive. But this is something that happens a great deal in Royal service.

He always felt that as Private Secretary he should be Number One when it came to giving any advice to the Prince. He resented the late Lord Mountbatten's influence enormously. He used to get furious when Lord Mountbatten interfered, and Lord Mountbatten interfered a lot.

Lord Mountbatten, the Prince's great-uncle, was also his honorary grandfather. They got on extremely well together. Prince Charles really loved the old gentleman, and was devastated by his assassination by the IRA. The course of British history might well have changed if Lord Mountbatten had lived. It was his dream that Prince Charles marry his granddaughter, Amanda Knatchbull. She is a sweet, quiet girl who is now training to become a social worker. Prince Charles never showed the slightest excitement when she was around. Other girls, particularly Lady Diana, made him sparkle and brought him to life. Not Amanda. But he was fond of her—he'd known her since she was a little girl.

Whenever the Prince went to Broadlands, Lord Mountbatten's home, lo and behold, there was Amanda invited over too. Lord Mountbatten was pushing, and what Lord Mountbatten wanted, he usually got. David Checketts was against the whole thing. He could see exactly what Lord Mountbatten was up to: he'd married off his nephew, Prince Philip, to the future Queen of England, and now he wanted to marry his granddaughter to the next King.

It would all have been suitable enough on paper, except that we felt it would look like an arranged marriage, with no love. What worried Staff, and Household even more, was that if we got Amanda, we got the whole Mountbatten family, the Brabournes and the Knatchbulls. We used to say at the Palace that if Lord Mountbatten won his slow, tenacious drip-drip battle, we wouldn't just inherit a Princess, we'd inherit ten Brabournes and Knatchbulls. None of Lord Mountbatten's family was exactly backward in coming forward; most of them were highly ambitious.

Perhaps I should explain here that Lord Mountbatten was born Prince Louis of Battenberg. He had married Edwina Ashley, who was at that time, during the 1920s, probably the richest woman in England. They had two daughters, Patricia and Pamela. Patricia married Lord Brabourne, a filmmaker, and Pamela married David Hicks, an interior decorator. The Brabournes (family name: Knatchbull) had seven children; the Hickses only two. Lord Mountbatten himself was a man of enormous charm, equally enormous vanity, and the most incredible energy. He nearly wore me out when we went to India with him.

While Lord Mountbatten liked to see himself as a kingmaker, he had a genuinely deep love for his grandnephew. Prince Philip had disappointed him by becoming cool towards him once he was the Queen's consort. Thereafter Mountbatten had showered his considerable knowledge, intelligence, and good old-fashioned common sense on Prince Charles.

"Uncle Dickie can get away with anything," Prince

Charles once said to me, shaking his head in admiration at Lord Mountbatten's cheek. "Did I ever tell you about the time he was going from Broadlands to an engagement in Southampton, and he was late, and speeding?"

I shook my head.

"Suddenly a traffic policeman roared up and stopped him," the Prince told me. "The man recognized him, but before he could say a word, Uncle Dickie said crossly, 'About bloody time too. I'm late. Now lead me into Southampton.'

"And the bemused traffic cop did as he was told."

The Prince relied on him for many things. Lord Mountbatten was his listening post, his confidant, his friend. The morning of Lord Mountbatten's funeral, Prince Charles put on every medal and every decoration he was entitled to wear on his naval uniform. Lord Mountbatten had always said to him, "If you've got it, wear it."

"If the IRA want to get me through the heart," the Prince said grimly, pinning on another medal, "they'll have a hard job."

I knew that they had already got him through the heart.

Lord Mountbatten wasn't the only one to die in that explosion at Classiebawn Castle on August 27, 1979. In the boat loaded with IRA explosives, Lord Mountbatten's grandson Nicholas Knatchbull died, aged just fourteen. A young Irish boatman died, and also the Dowager Lady Brabourne, who was in her eighties.

Lady Brabourne, Lord Mountbatten's daughter, was on a life-support machine for weeks. Once she was well again, she told the Prince of her experience.

"She could hear," Prince Charles said to me, his voice awed. "She could understand every word that was being said, but she couldn't move a muscle to tell anyone that her brain was still working."

The Prince was fascinated by what Lady Brabourne had described as an out-of-body experience while she was so close to death. He is terrifically interested in reincarnation and spiritualism. Indeed, he is convinced that the next time he comes back to earth, it will be as someone important!

All this, of course, was before Lady Diana came on the scene. And I do wonder what Lord Mountbatten would have done if he had been alive and seen Amanda's chances receding. Some say the Prince actually did propose to her. Personally, I really don't believe it.

There was never any breath of a love affair that I was aware of. Indeed, he treated her like the cousin that she was, but then, he was so discreet. He never had a secret assignation spot, like the house where Princess Margaret and Lord Snowdon used to meet before they were married. And he picked girlfriends who were as discreet as he was himself.

While I was in Canada promoting my last book, *Royal Service*, my phone rang one night in Toronto. It was Janet Jenkins, one of Prince Charles's girlfriends whom I had liked very much and got to know quite well.

"Could I have a copy of the book?" she asked me. "I'm told I'm in it."

She was. I asked her over to my hotel for a drink and gave her a copy.

"Do you know," she said to me that night, "I wrote to Prince Charles when I heard he was marrying, and asked if he would like back all the letters I had received from him. He said 'No,' and that I should keep them. Wasn't that marvelous?"

It was marvelous. It confirmed my feeling that the Prince has always been brilliant at picking charming, pretty, exciting girls—who knew how to keep their mouths shut.

THE WALES FAMILY

Chapter Six

TRAVELING
ROYALLY

ONE NICE THING ABOUT WORKING FOR ROYALTY, PROVIDED YOU are fairly high up in the pecking order, is that you get to travel. Free. And first class.

I most certainly did, in my years with Prince Charles. I don't think I missed a continent, and not a lot of countries, apart from Russia. My travels with him gave me a great love for the United States and Australia, neither of which I would ever have got to know so well if I hadn't had the amazing good luck to become his valet.

The Royals themselves are a little on the blasé side about overseas travel, and one can hardly blame them. The Queen must have lost count of the times she has been to Australia and New Zealand; Prince Charles would rather be at Balmoral than anywhere else in the world. Only the Duke of Edinburgh continues to globe-trot to such a degree that we used to think he should be dizzy, suffering from permanent jet lag.

But it would not be true to say that there are many Royal long faces at the thought of a trip. All of them are delighted if they can land a tour or an independence ceremony in some nicely hot country during the depths of the British winter.

These official engagements are basically arranged by the Foreign Office, liaising with the Royal Household. Twice a year the Royals themselves hold a meeting at the Palace, and all the visits—dull or exciting—are divided up. The list is worked out on a huge board which hangs in the Equerries' Office. This board shows at a glance where each member of the family will be in the next six months, plus the method of transportation. The board is locked up each night for obvious security reasons.

The program includes home engagements as well, and on these care must be taken that there are no clashes. When a Royal visits one of the British counties, the Lord Lieutenant of that county has to greet him or her. On one occasion somebody boobed, and Prince Charles and Prince Philip were both visiting different ends of the same county on the same day. The poor unfortunate Lord Lieutenant was rushing from one place to another in a state of dementia.

Of course, the overseas trips cost the Royals nothing. If an engagement happens to be taking place at a spot not far from some area in which they have a personal interest, there is keen competition for the job. Princess Margaret has achieved gold status when it comes to freeloading her way to the Caribbean. Since her house is on the island of Mustique, she is always on the lookout for a lift in that general direction. The result—she has given goodness knows how many of the islands their independence, the last one being St. Kitts, in 1983, from which she promptly flew to Mustique for an extracurricular holiday. What she is going to do for that ride when Britain has given away all the Caribbean, heaven only knows.

The Prince of Wales is not above such tactics. If he wants to go to the Bahamas, or to play polo in Miami, he'll fix himself a visit to Canada or Venezuela, to cut down on the fares. And one of his friends, the American tycoon Dr. Armand Hammer, is always happy to send one of his planes.

Not all the foreign jobs are so popular. No one wanted to give Zimbabwe its independence in 1980. There was a lot of guerilla warfare going on, and for this reason, it was decided that the Queen could not possibly go. The job was passed to Prince Charles.

As it happened, we had a marvelous time, mainly because Sir Christopher Soames, Winston Churchill's son-in-law, was the acting governor. The Soameses are great friends of the Prince. We stayed with them in a bungalow in the grounds of Government House, which has now become the Presidential Palace. Nothing serious happened. Though there was a bomb threat on the night of the actual ceremony, nothing came of it.

We didn't see much of Zimbabwe, I'm afraid, but then, we never saw much of anywhere.

In 1983 Princess Anne's husband, Mark Phillips, was going to Australia to compete in some equestrian events and also to do some training. They are both horse-mad, and Princess Anne wanted to go with him, but the fare to Australia is not inconsiderable. Her private secretary rang the Foreign Office to say that the Princess would be available to go to Australia on a Royal tour at that time if Australia were interested.

Unfortunately for Princess Anne, they were not. The word came back from the F.O. that if she was keen to go they would pencil her in for a trip in several years' time. Last year they had Princess Diana and Prince Charles. Since the Government in office is socialist, they had probably had enough of Royals for a while.

Another reason could have been that the host country bears the expense of a Royal visit; it doesn't cost the Royals themselves a cent. And a tour can be very expensive. In the old days, when I traveled with the Prince we all stuck it out, good and bad, until the end of the tour. Now they change staff in midstream if the tour is a long one. That means more expense—double the air fares. And everyone travels first class. Princess Diana even changed her hairdresser after three weeks of her Australian tour, flying one back, and bringing out another.

Incidentally, I have a theory about how Princess Anne finally got her trip and joined her husband. She agreed—a most unusual thing—to do an interview on Australian television with Michael Parkinson, the top British TV interviewer. Her expenses to Australia were paid, but her fee was given to the Save the Children Fund, with expenses off the top. The TV program was a great success, and probably to her astonishment, Princess Anne found herself enormously popular—perhaps for the first time since she was a curl-topped, golden-haired toddler.

Most of the time Royalty travel in their own private transport and there is quite a lot to choose from. The Royal Yacht, three Andovers of the Queen's Flight, two bright red helicopters (one usually annexed by the Duke of Edinburgh, who loves to fly himself), a couple of VC10s provided by the RAF for longer distances, and their favorite, the Royal Train. All of these are basically paid for by the British taxpayer.

For any journey near home, the Queen travels by car. She has a fleet of cars, usually Fords, most of which are hired at very advantageous rates, the Ford Company recognizing a bit of good PR when they see it.

She herself always travels in the old green Rover which I have already mentioned, or a splendid Rolls without a license plate. Whether she is traveling alone, or with her entire entourage following, the Queen is not one for moving about with a motorcycle escort. She prefers to travel quietly and less obtrusively.

For official journeys, policemen are stationed at intersections along the entire route and, as her car approaches, all other traffic is momentarily halted. This is done for all members of the family. Ex–Prime Minister Heath was foolish enough to complain recently because the passing of the Queen Mother's car held him up, and he was thus too late to cast his vote at the close of a debate in the House of Commons. Since the British public have a lot more interest in the Queen Mother than in the Right Honorable Edward Heath, he got short shrift.

On less official journeys, the Royals move as simply as possible. When the Queen goes off to Windsor for the weekend, there will be a chauffeur and a detective in the front seats of the Rover, while she will be in the back, with as many corgis as possible stuffed in beside her.

The top form of transportation is the Royal Train, which was completely refurbished in 1977, ready for the Queen's Jubilee, when she would be traveling constantly around the country. The train is kept in a siding at Wolverton, Buckinghamshire, in the Home Counties. While the work was going on, Prince Philip was always rushing up the M1 motorway to keep an eye on progress.

The work was meant to cost £100,000. It finished up costing half a million pounds, instead, and there were a lot of grumbles from the political left in Parliament. In fact, as Prince Charles said, it did need some improvements, though he personally was disappointed it had been made so modern. The wooden carriages that were replaced were 1940 vintage.

"The Queen swears they have square wheels," Prince Charles used to say.

The new train has two special day salons, one for the Queen and one for Prince Philip, which the British press noted sardonically as "his and hers." There was speculation as to whether they couldn't bear to sit together in the same room.

"It really is unfair," Prince Charles grumbled. "They don't

accept that the Queen is working, even when she is on the train."

The Queen's own coach has a formal entrance, double doors, lounge, bedroom and bathroom, with a separate bedroom and bathroom for her dresser. The Duke has much the same arrangement, only slightly smaller and with a shower instead of a bath.

The Queen and Prince Philip chose the curtains, carpets, and built-in sofas that were provided with the refit, but the rest of the furniture was brought from Buckingham Palace.

Of course, there is more than one Royal Train, as it is quite possible for the Queen to be going, say, to Newcastle, while the Prince of Wales will be going to Cornwall. This is when the Royal pecking order comes into evidence. The Number One Royal Train and crew go with the Queen and Prince Philip. Prince Charles gets the Number Two, which he never minds a bit as he prefers the old-fashioned rolling stock. He thinks the old carriages are much cozier than the modern choice of his father.

If, by chance, three Royal trains are running on the same night, or the entire family are going up to Balmoral together, Princess Anne and the rest of the family get the really ancient rolling stock and an out-of-practice crew.

No one in the family gets uppity about this. They are all aware that the Queen is the fountainhead, and that one day Prince Charles will be. The rest of them are actually rather relieved and grateful that the burden of Monarchy will never fall on them. If the disadvantage of being low in the pecking order means accommodation in the least of the Royal railway carriages, they don't mind at all.

I'll never forget the first trip I made on the newly fitted-out Royal Train. We were all coming back from the summer holiday in Balmoral. The Queen, Prince Charles, Princess Margaret—nearly all the family were aboard.

In the train one gets from one end to the other by corridors, but the Queen's sitting room is open plan. While the staff were putting luggage on board, the Queen was saying her usual dignified farewell to the stationmaster and thanking him for being there—all traditional Royal protocol. Prince Charles was using his father's rooms on the train, and I had to go through the Queen's sitting room to get into them with his personal belongings. As I went through, there she was—the Queen who had been saying gracious farewells just a minute before—down on her hands and knees, headscarf on, putting down spread-out copies of *The Times* and *Financial Times* to cover the new beige carpet.

"Excuse me, Your Majesty," I said as I edged past her.

She looked up. "Oh, hallo, Stephen," she said. "I'm just putting these down for the dogs."

I could see her point. She could hardly take them "walkies" from a moving train.

Prince Charles is very funny about the Royal Train. He actually gets annoyed if he can't have his old-fashioned carriages. For one thing, he hates showers. He likes to wallow in a bath, and the modern train only has a shower, built to his father's orders.

When we were using the train for out-of-London engagements, the Prince always came back to his own carriage for a bath and to change after the work was over. And there we would be, sitting on a siding somewhere, surrounded by a ring of security. Inside the train, the Prince would be happily relaxing in a hot, foamy bath. Outside, the security staff would see a stream of bubbles floating along the track when I finally let the water run out. Across the way could be steel mills, coal mines, factories; on this little stretch of railway line, a Royal Prince would be taking a nice bath, with hot towels waiting, and his clothing laid out all ready to be put on.

Mad!

If we were on the train for more than two days, we took along an old racing bicycle, too. The Prince, who is pretty fanatical about keeping fit, would take this out when we were at a siding and cycle round the country lanes, his policeman panting behind.

The Royal Train causes chaos on the rail networks, just as the Royal carriages hold up traffic in London. We would be whizzing along at a hundred miles an hour, and we would see commuter trains, wedged with people, the windows steamed up and the passengers equally steamed up, waiting to get going again. They would have no idea that the Queen or Prince Charles was passing by, as we sat there in great comfort drinking our morning tea.

There is always another engine running about a mile ahead of the Royal Train to clear the way, and to be sure that nothing is on the track. So, not surprisingly, I can't remember an occasion when anything ever went wrong.

It used to amuse me when we went to Kings Cross Station, where the Royal Train always leaves from for Balmoral. The Royals arrive in a fleet of cars and park on Platform One, where it is possible to get straight onto the train without going through the station concourse. The only problem is that Platform One is also used by the post office vans. Post office workers are rarely an ardent Royalist lot. As the Royals thread their way through mounds of parcels, newspapers, and post bags, getting in the way of the workers, there is a certain amount of muttered abuse as the men try to load and unload Her Majesty's Mail.

I loved traveling on the Royal Train, and even the Royals regard it as a "perk." British Rail does the best breakfasts in the world, and they also have superb wine cellars.

"Why is it," the Prince used to say, "that the Palace chefs need an acre of space to boil an egg, and the British Rail chefs create a superb breakfast in a cupboard?"

At the Palace the Prince never ate breakfast, but he always ordered it on the train.

"Well, it's fun," he used to say.

The staff on the train are hand-picked from the regions. When I was in Royal service, the chef had been seconded from British Rail's crack Pullman service. He, like the others who travel with Royalty, was basically just an ordinary British Rail chef, but to watch him and his colleagues at work as the train rattles along, coping with boiling pans and keeping delicate sauces going, is quite a sight. It looks dangerous, but somehow they never seem to burn themselves.

The bright red Royal Helicopters follow the Royal Train in popularity, and are allowed to break some of the rules governing ordinary helicopter travel. For example, in London private helicopters are supposed to follow the line of the River Thames and not fly over the city itself. Royal Helicopters are exempt from this rule.

The Royals like this mode of transport because it is so convenient. The Queen Mother, regardless of advancing age, is never long out of one.

The Queen is the unfortunate one. She is not allowed to fly in helicopters or single-engine aircraft, a rule imposed by the Home Office under the Safety of the Sovereign regulations. This has been broken only twice—once when she went to Northern Ireland on her first helicopter trip, which she loathed, and again for the Fortieth Anniversary of D-Day celebrations.

In terrorist-torn Northern Ireland it was much more secure to take her everywhere by helicopter. If anything had gone wrong, they could have whisked her away quickly. And only in a helicopter could she have reviewed the D-Day landing beaches.

Whenever the Royals fly, they are given a "purple" (that is, Royalty) priority air route by the ground traffic controllers. In 1981 Prince Philip, who loves to fly himself, caused the most terrific upset in Britain when an Andover of the Queen's Flight narrowly missed a Miami-bound British Airways Boeing 747 as it was climbing at three hundred miles per hour away from Gatwick Airport.

The jumbo's captain said that an unidentified black object shot across in front of him in heavy cloud over Surrey. It was on a Friday afternoon. It took three days before the Palace would admit that Prince Philip had been at the controls, flying under his special call sign, Rainbow Task. He was 1,000 feet too low, missing the "purple" corridor completely on his way to Gatwick. He was a mile ahead of the jumbo—ten seconds' flying time. Though the 747 captain had to take avoiding action, fortunately no harm was done.

Prince Philip was sixty at the time, five years older than Britain permits her commercial pilots to be. Since the jumbo had been carrying two hundred and sixty passengers and they were only seconds from disaster, the British public put it down to arrogance when it took so long for the Palace to admit that Prince Philip had been at fault.

His press office finally said blandly, "We didn't deny he was at the controls. We didn't confirm, which is a different thing altogether." What everyone missed was that—since the incident happened on a Friday afternoon, just as the Royals and the Household were off on their sacrosanct weekend—no one would get any information out of the Palace until the following week.

I was working at the Palace at that time; nothing was ever said about the incident. But, then, nothing was ever said about any Royal misdemeanor. If Princess Anne got a speeding ticket, Princess Diana a parking ticket, or Prince Andrew caused a scandal with an actress—it never happened as far as the Royals are concerned. They completely ignore these little hiccups in the even tenor of their days.

Of course, they have little need to worry much about anything. I remember Prince Charles and I were flying together to Scotland, one time, in the Andover. I went to see him in his study, and said, "Sir, you do realize we ought to be going?"

"Why?" he asked.

"Because, sir," I told him, "it is eleven, and the plane leaves at twelve."

"Keep calm, Stephen. Don't worry," he said. "They won't go without me."

THE ROYAL YACHT *BRITANNIA* IS ALSO A MUCH-FAVORED FORM of Royal transport, though the taxpayer in Britain is heard to moan about the cost. In 1982, at the time of the Falklands war, there were definite rumblings of discontent. It had been announced that the Royal Yacht would not be used as a hospital ship, though this is meant to be her wartime navy role.

The rumblings were even louder when the *Canberra* was taken off a cruise and sent to the South Atlantic instead, so that people's holidays had to be postponed or canceled. The official reason given was that the *Britannia* used the wrong type of fuel and could not have been refueled that far from home base. An excuse that wasn't entirely convincing, though it was the truth.

As an ex-sailor, the Duke of Edinburgh is particularly fond of traveling in the yacht. And it is "in," not "on." I was always saying "on" to Prince Charles, who would firmly correct me. "Stephen," he would say, "it is *in* the yacht we are about to travel. Not *on* it."

It is the largest yacht in the world. It has a crew of two hundred and seventy-seven. The Queen takes her own Staff when she is on board. All the other Royals use the naval crew, who are terrifically efficient.

The yacht is a royal-blue floating palace. Built in 1953, it is four hundred twelve feet long, and costs an estimated £3,000,000 a year to run. All the Royal apartments are aft, spread over three decks. The top deck contains the Royal bedrooms and bathrooms, of which there are four, all with large single beds. The main deck supports a drawing room which can hold two hundred people. It even has a fireplace!

Also on this deck is the dining room, which seats up to sixty people. This doubles as the cinema, as the Queen likes to watch a movie when she is on board.

Below are at least twenty Household cabins, which are also used by extra members of the Royal family when on board. The decks are linked by an elevator, which is to be avoided in rough seas.

The Staff are housed below, in forty cabins, that are missing paneling and have never been properly completed, as the company fitting out the yacht was on strike when she was launched.

There are two small, cozier sitting rooms on the main deck, which the Queen and the Duke use when they are alone. They like to take their breakfast on the verandah deck, overlooking the stern. This verandah was highly popular with the Prince and Princess of Wales, who spent most of their honeymoon days there, relaxing in the sun. They sit in solitary state in the dining room for other meals.

Curiously, up until recently, the *Britannia* was the only ship afloat in which some sailors still slept in hammocks. Since the refit, they now all have beds. There is also cabin space for the Queen's Marine Band, all thirty of them, whom she often takes on overseas visits.

The *Britannia* has a garage on board, in case the Queen wishes to take her own Rolls-Royce with her. But this is more often used to store beer for the crew, on longer voyages. Apart from all the magnificence, the thing that most impressed me when I sailed on the Waleses' honeymoon with them was the cleanliness of the entire ship. It really would not have been a hardship to eat off the floors.

The Duke uses the *Britannia* at Cowes as a floating home for his yearly sailing regatta week there. The Prince and Princess Diana used it for their honeymoon, as I told in *Royal Service*. It is the Queen's floating palace for many overseas tours, as when she used it on her official tour to California in 1983.

I felt for her, knowing just how the Royal Yacht can rock and roll. The stabilizers are not effective, and the weather the Queen encountered in California was unusually dreadful. Storms, rain, wind, rough seas—everything was guaranteed to make life in a ship uncomfortable. But, British to the end, the *Britannia* was still host to a fantastic party for the Reagans.

It is not just glamorous places like California that the *Britannia* visits. She sails once a year, with the Queen Mother aboard, from Dover on the south coast round to the seven Cinque Ports. These are ancient British ports: Sandwich and Rye (which are both inland now), Romney, Dover, Hastings, Hythe, and Winchelsea—which, by tradition dating from before the Norman Conquest, have a Lord Warden.

Churchill held this post after the Second World War. On his death Sir Robert Menzies, the former Australian prime minister, took over. Today the Queen Mother—the first woman ever—holds the position. It is something she is particularly proud of, since being Lord Warden is a great honor. And she is, of course, always royally entertained by whichever of the ports is her host.

In Rye she was taken from the yacht to lunch at the historic Mermaid Inn, a fine old hotel, reputedly heavily haunted. She made the young manager's week by returning after she had said goodbye, to say, "This is such a charming hotel. I do wish I was staying."

Perhaps the sea wasn't too calm that day!

When the Royal Family travel, they don't just take piles of luggage. They arrive with records, record player, fishing rods, shotguns, videotapes, photographs, books, chocolates, sometimes even their favorite trinkets. They like wherever they stay to look homey. They even move the film projector between Balmoral and Sandringham. The pipe major doubles as projectionist.

Prince Charles always carried a silver-framed photograph of the Queen, and also of Princess Alexandra, his favorite cousin. For a while, before he married, he also treasured a casual snapshot of Lady Diana (as she was then), which he kept beside his bed. Today his favorite photograph of her, which is kept framed at Highgrove, is one he took on the Royal honeymoon. In it she is laughing, and wearing a skimpy green bikini.

When the Queen travels, most of her good jewelry travels with her. She never moves without it. The Royal jewelry has its own suitcase, made of heavy brown leather, protected by a canvas cover with the words "The Queen" printed on the outside in black type. It is approximately thirty inches long, by twenty inches deep and ten inches wide. It is large! But, then, so is the fabled Royal collection that it houses. Even so, this case does not hold all the Queen's jewelry. She travels only with her favorite pieces. The rest are safely locked up in an impregnable safe in her own apartments. It is her footman's job to carry this Queen's fortune, and not unnaturally, the responsibility gives him the tremors.

The jewelry includes pieces like the Queen's favorite set of diamonds, which was given to her by the South African government on her twenty-first birthday. There are also three strings of huge diamonds, with earrings to match. She also carries Queen Victoria's Jubilee necklace of diamonds and pearls. Her emeralds are from Brazil, a gift from the President and the people of Brazil on her Coronation. Her rubies came from the King and Queen on her wedding day. All this goes to both Balmoral and Sandringham, along with assorted tiaras; the Queen rarely travels without a tiara.

Despite staff vigilance, accidents can happen. Once, at Windsor, Bobo misread the jewelry program list furnished for all Royals by the Lord Chamberlain's office. She missed the T for Tiara, realized too late, and had to borrow one from the Queen's lady-in-waiting. Absurd, when you think that the Queen has about twenty of her own.

She also travels with a special dressing case that contains

all her makeup. This is Bobo's responsibility, and when they are going off anywhere, Bobo is inclined to look as if the brown leather case has grown onto her hand, so used are we to seeing her with it.

Each member of the Royal Family has his or her own identifying colored luggage label on each piece of baggage. The Queen's labels are yellow, the Duke of Edinburgh's mauve, Prince Charles's red, Princess Anne's green—and so it goes. There is a sensible reason for this. When traveling abroad, particularly in the Third World, Royals very often find the hotel porters and other help cannot read. The colored labels make it easier.

All this travel makes for a lot of packing and unpacking for the staff. And this is more complex than you might think, particularly after the summer holiday at Balmoral. A week before we leave, after the ten-week stay, the packing begins. Silver and china have to be carefully made ready to return unbroken to the Palace.

My particular job after we stayed at Craigowan was to go down to the cellars to get the booze. They buy spirits on arrival in Aberdeen, but anything left over is taken back to the Palace, even if it is only half a bottle. And that half-bottle is recorded on what is called the Drinks Book, kept by the Yeoman of the Cellar. The Deputy Master of the Household eventually checks on this to make sure that no one has been helping himself to the Monarch's alcohol.

At the end of this long Balmoral holiday, the staff endeavor to get the night train back to London to see their families as soon as possible. They attempt to go immediately after the Queen herself has left, so they like to get on with the packing as quickly as possible.

One morning Christopher Bray, the Queen's Page, who took over from Bennett, was on duty when the Queen asked to see the piece of silver she was taking on a Royal tour as a gift. He went off to look, took ages, came back, and said,

"I'm so sorry, Your Majesty, but it's been packed. The silver pantry didn't think you'd want to see it again for the moment."

A little later she rang again. "Perhaps you could bring me the books from the sitting room," she said. The Queen has a thing about distributing books all around the guests' rooms.

Christopher, somewhat crestfallen, said, "I'm sorry, Your Majesty. I've started packing again. It'll just take me a few minutes to get them out for you."

About half an hour later she rang for Christopher yet again. "Perhaps you could ring Purvey for me and ask for my Land-Rover to be brought round," she said, adding, "That is, of course, if he hasn't packed it."

Sometimes things that have been packed cause considerable problems. On a Royal tour, the female secretary chosen to travel is in charge of the stationery boxes and the presents that the Royals will give to their hosts. I can remember occasions when we were traveling and there would suddenly be a frightful panic. God knows how many thousand feet up over Africa, or somewhere, the secretary would suddenly realize that the present the Prince meant to hand over on arrival was in the aircraft's hold.

"I'm afraid it will have to be got out," the Prince would say on being informed, usually by me, of this misadventure. This meant that some poor devil from the crew had to pull up the plane's carpet, climb down through the hatch into the hold, find the right box, and, with luck, bring up the right article. It wasn't particularly dangerous, but it was not a very pleasant task, and whoever had boobed in packing was decidedly unpopular with the crew.

The present is almost always a silver salver. Solid silver, of course. And, to tell the truth, generally a recycled one. The Royals have dozens and dozens of silver salvers that have been presented to them over the years, and with the silver being solid it is quite easy to remove the engraving and start again.

The Royals don't consider themselves either givers or receivers of presents personally. They are presenting on behalf of the nation and receiving on behalf of the nation, so if the Queen does a bit of recycling it can only be good for the taxpayer.

The Queen's stock phrase as she hands over her gift is always, "It's rather small, but I hope you like it." And it is small, compared with the booty that the oil sheikhs handed over to her on her Middle Eastern trip in 1979. Their gifts were astronomically valuable. Their generosity was amazing. Most of the gift articles were made of solid gold and of the most beautiful workmanship, invariably French. She got so many priceless things that the problem was where to put them. In the end some found a home on the Royal Yacht, which is now a floating museum full of exquisite things.

A smaller-scale copy of an Arab dhow, made in silver fretwork, is displayed in the yacht's dining room. But the most spectacular gift was a miniature oasis consisting of a pair of solid gold palm trees with two gold camels standing beneath. The coconuts hanging from the palms are made of gold rubies, the size of grapes. The sailors on board go by, shake them gently, and say, "If one falls, is it mine?"

The Royals receive astonishing presents all the time. One morning I found a note from the Prince's office saying there was a boat for him in the Windsor Royal Mews. A gift, they said, from Madame Marcos, wife of the Philippines President.

"I suppose it will be a rowing boat," the Prince said when I told him, but we hotfooted it over there as soon as possible to have a look. It turned out to be the most enormous twin-engined speedboat. There was one snag: It had no engines.

"I suppose she just said to her embassy, 'Buy a boat,' "

the Prince said gloomily, looking at this enormous, useless piece of equipment. "We'd better find out how much the engines cost."

The answer was £36,000. The Prince would never spend that much on something he didn't really need. In the end, he had a brilliant idea. He gave the boat to a youth organization, and the Queen's Jubilee Appeal paid for the engines.

Madame Marcos was always sending him presents. Once it was ten volumes of her travels, consisting mostly of photographs of her arrivals in different places, surrounded by people in dark glasses.

He was also sent some very glitzy cufflinks, all gold and diamonds. These came from an Arab prince. He looked at them when I presented them to him and shook his head.

"They're not quite me," he said.

Indeed, they were not.

His secretary, Michael Colborne, had an "in" with Mappin and Webb, the jewelers, so it was decided that Michael should take the cufflinks along and get them valued. Back came the word that they were worth £11,000.

The Prince was overjoyed. "A new polo pony and something towards the girl grooms' wages," he said. "I shall sell them."

Unfortunately, the next move in the game was an apologetic letter from Mappin. They had got it wrong; the cufflinks were worth only a thousand pounds. The Prince decided they were not worth selling. They are still around somewhere, until they get recycled in their turn.

The gift-giving isn't confined just to gifts for the Royal Family. On overseas tours, the Household and Staff often receive presents from the host country, usually a watch or jewelry of some kind. The pages and footmen look forward to a large tip or present. It makes overseas trips vied for by the staff as, certainly in some countries, they are showered with gifts. The same happens with distinguished visitors to Britain. When the late Shah came to Windsor, there was great competition among the footmen as to who would see him off the premises. His aides would tip with gold coins from Iran.

The Queen, of course, is informed by Bobo about who is getting what. One night at dinner in Saudi Arabia she said to Prince Philip, "I've just been on the phone to Mummy, who tells me that the Customs strike is still on at home. Good news for some, I thought, with all their lovely presents." The footman at the table had a hard time keeping a straight face.

When the Prince and I used to travel, we always carried a great many medals for giving as gifts. In Nepal, for the King's coronation, we were handing out Coronation medals like candy. "It's much cheaper than a present," the Prince would say, "but it means a lot more to the recipient."

And that was true.

Moving the Royals from one place to another is a bit of a circus, and they do not appreciate other people's problems in getting from A to B. For them there is always a car waiting, a helicopter hovering, or a plane poised on the runway. Off they go, while the rest of us can be desperately trying to find a car to keep up.

Also, they never suffer from jet lag, as they always have a bed made up for them on the plane. I remember, in Rio, jet lag got me. Prince Charles and I had arrived at the hotel, I had seen that he was comfortable and organized, and I went to my room and just lay down for a minute's rest. But the minute stretched to five hours.

The next thing I knew, there was a great banging on the hotel room door. It was a member of the hotel security staff. "The Prince is looking everywhere for you," he said, as, bleary-eyed, I opened the door. I pulled myself together and rushed to the Prince's suite in a cold sweat. I found him looking a bit forlorn.

"Where have you been?" he said. "Where's my dinner?"

Well, I'd been asleep and his dinner was late. I'd forgotten all about it. He was grumpy, pulling his "you've-let-me-down" face, which could always make me feel guilty.

Hotels, particularly in big cities, are the worst. I was always being put on a completely different floor from the Prince, and then had to wait for the elevator to come up twenty floors to take me to him. That can take fifteen minutes, if you're unlucky. What makes it worse is that one elevator is always set aside for Royal use, making the others more crowded.

Not a great deal goes wrong on overseas tours, though, because an awful lot happens behind the scenes that the Royals never see. At least six weeks before any one of them visits another country, or even a town in Britain, many security arrangements are made. The Traveling Yeoman, a private secretary, a press secretary, and the personal detective completely cover the exact route that will be taken. They check out hotels by staying in them, and transport by riding in it, not only for comfort but for safety as well, for the Queen and for the sixty or so people who always travel with her. The same precautions are taken for Prince Charles and Princess Diana—indeed, for all top Royals, though their entourages are much smaller.

Thank God, except for one deranged young man who fired blank bullets at the Queen in 1981, when she was performing the Trooping of the Color ceremony, there has never been even a near-tragedy while the Royals have been in a public situation. Ironically, the most terrible tragedy of all—the death of Lord Mountbatten, who was assassinated by the IRA—happened while he was on holiday. He was in Ireland, which he loved, and staying at his own home, where he spent every summer.

I myself did quite a bit of traveling with Lord Mountbatten. He and the Prince used to love to go off together, and I would act as valet to them both. India, where Lord Mountbatten had been Viceroy, was a place where he was still treated like a god, and he was thrilled to show his great-nephew the scenes of his earlier triumphs. He was with us in Nepal for the coronation of its King. One morning he came to see Prince Charles.

"Do you need Stephen?" he asked.

Prince Charles, thinking he wanted some help, said, "No." (They do lend out staff like a commodity.) But Mountbatten didn't want help. He wanted company. He put me in the back of a huge car owned by the Nepalese government and took me off to a palace.

"The last time I was here," he said, "was with the *last* Prince of Wales. When I think how long it took us to get here in those days! We came by horseback, and the present [Nepalese] King's grandfather pointed proudly to his chest, where, even at this hour and in these informal circumstances, he was in full naval uniform and wearing every decoration he had."

That was so different from Prince Charles's cousin, the quiet young architect Prince Richard, Duke of Gloucester, who was also at the coronation. The Duke of Gloucester had been at Eton in England with the new King, and he and his Duchess, Birgitte, had come to Nepal for the ceremonies. The Duchess is a Danish girl the Duke met at Cambridge University, and they are an unpretentious couple. At the coronation she was ironing her own dresses and setting her own hair, as the Gloucesters are the least well-off of the Royals. They were also in Nepal privately, so most likely they did not benefit from another Royal perk. What the public doesn't know is that every time a top Royal takes an official trip abroad, the visit carries with it a large dress allowance from the Foreign Office.

The Prince's accountant would ring me when we were off somewhere, and ask: "Will he require any uniforms for this trip?" As the Prince has around forty uniforms, most of them hardly ever worn, the answer is invariably, "No."

The office would then suggest, "Why don't we get a couple of suits and some shirts instead?" So we did, and sent the bill to the Foreign Office and, indirectly, the taxpayer. But then everybody, down to the kitchen porter (in the unlikely event of his being wanted on an overseas tour), gets a new suit if going abroad.

The Prince did pay me a clothing allowance. Obviously, I always had to look reasonably well dressed, as I was just two paces behind him most of the time. But I'm afraid the allowance didn't cover my dress expenses completely.

The Royal Family are, I fear, as tight as a Scotsman's purse, so I never really bothered to explain that I was out of pocket. It wouldn't have made any difference.

Chapter Seven

A PRIDE OF PRINCESSES

"I CANNOT UNDERSTAND," THE QUEEN SAID ONE DAY WHEN the Royals were up in Balmoral on holiday, "why the Staff are always so tired. It's ridiculous."

She was speaking to Bennett, her page, who took a deep breath and his courage in his hands, and said, "Well, it's Princess Margaret, ma'am."

"What do you mean, 'It's Princess Margaret?' " the Queen asked sharply.

As he was in for a penny, Bennett decided he might as well be in for a pound, and continued, "She keeps everyone up so late, ma'am. She doesn't go to bed until three and they can't go before she gives her permission. Then they do have to get up at seven, ma'am."

"I see," said the Queen, looking thoughtful.

Later that week, so that it didn't look too obvious that she had taken notice of servants' gossip, she issued a directive to Staff that once she herself had gone to bed, usually around midnight, the rest of the family would look after themselves. The rest of the family meant just Princess Margaret. She is the night owl of the Royals, the only one who stays up after the Queen has retired. Bed never attracts her; she will stay up until all hours.

This owl temperament of hers is equally tiresome for guests. If they don't make the move quickly when the Queen says good night, they are stuck until the Princess decides to go to bed. No one slides off while Royalty is in the room, a fact that gives the Princess something of a captive audience for her late-night playing and singing at the piano. While the Staff might be tired, waiting to go to bed, sometimes the guests are equally so.

Her own Staff become resigned, but at Balmoral and Sandringham, Princess Margaret is looked after by the Queen's Staff, who do not. The only people of her own that she travels with are her dresser and a police officer. Arriving and departing, she is always collected and accompanied by her chauffeur and a lady-in-waiting.

Her own Staff, back in Kensington Palace, where she lives in a three-story apartment, never really get used to the odd hours she keeps. She has a chef, kitchen help, a butler, an under-butler, and a lot of "dailies." Her apartment is on the south side of the palace, which is overlooked by the Royal Garden Hotel. Guests there can sometimes spot her sunbathing, much to her annoyance. The Queen's gardens are overlooked too, by the Hilton, but the Queen does not sunbathe.

For many years Princess Margaret had a butler called Richard, who put up with a great deal from her. Until the day he exploded. For some weeks she had been going out at night, to the theater or to concerts and on to nightclubs. She had fallen into the habit of arriving home well after midnight and bringing a whole party of people with her.

Imperiously she would ring the bell and sweep in, demanding supper for all. She is the only member of the Royal Family to carry keys, but she is always losing them. She often has to use them when she is so late that the Staff have given up in despair and gone to bed. On these impromptu-party nights, Richard would be rushing around trying to rustle up something from the refrigerator, knowing that the chef would be irritated the next morning when he found it had been raided.

The last straw came on the night of the Queen Mother's birthday, when Princess Margaret said casually to Richard, "We shall be six for dinner at eleven-thirty." And not another word.

Via the Palace, Richard learned that the casual six were in fact the Queen Mother, the Queen and Prince Philip, Lord Snowdon, and Prince Charles. He was furious. With such guests, both he and the Staff would want to do everything perfectly, particularly for the Queen Mother on her birthday.

From his staff room in the basement he heard them come back that night, and then the sound of feet in the flagstone hall. Princess Margaret had let herself and her guests in. The detectives and the chauffeurs came downstairs. "Why are you down here?" they were asking. "Her Majesty's upstairs."

"No one told *me*," he said.

Eventually, Princess Margaret rang through on the inter-house telephone, and said, "Richard, we're back." Still angry, and with no sense of urgency, he went to see the chef and prepared to serve the dinner. Eventually he came to the drawing room and, wooden-faced, said, "Dinner is served, Your Royal Highness," and turned to leave.

"We'd better go in, Lillibet," he heard the Princess say to the Queen, "or there'll be the most frightful row."

Their relationship continued to be stormy. On one occasion he threatened to leave, and trying to make him look dispensable, she said, "If you're going, have you a friend who would like to work here in beautiful surroundings, serving in a beautiful dining room?"

"I'm afraid," said Richard coldly, "my friends want dining rooms of their own." On another occasion when she had upset him, he told her firmly that he wanted to go, and he meant it.

"Well," she said, huge blue eyes fixed on him, "if you're going, I'm going, too."

Needless to say, he stayed on longer than planned.

People find Princess Margaret difficult because one moment she is friendly and laughing, almost flirtatious; the next minute she is freezing the room with a stare, and has suddenly become more Royal than the Queen. No one would ever get away with calling her anything but "ma'am."

The staff know only too well that, for all her mood changes, never can they presume for one moment, though there are times when they can almost get away with more than her friends would dare. And yet it was Princess Margaret who went to Liverpool, in the northwest of England, and was so dismayed by the unemployment in the area that she came back and persuaded the Queen to recruit Staff from there. Already several young Liverpudlians have started work at the Palace.

The Princess is a curious mixture of many things, maybe because her life has not been particularly happy. She was such a pretty woman, even when I first went to the Palace fourteen years ago. But fate has not been kind to her. She was not able to marry the man she loved as a young girl, Group Captain Peter Townsend. When she finally told the British people she would renounce him, she said the reason was that she was "ever mindful of the Church's teaching." Because Princess Margaret, for all her fascination with show business and show business people and despite her divorce, is deeply religious. More so than anyone else in the family with the exception of the Duchess of Kent, who goes on pilgrimages.

The Queen's sister is the most controversial of the family and is not always as thoughtful as she might be. One of the footmen tells the story of how Princess Margaret once took a small party to a gala at Covent Garden Opera House.

Princess Margaret and her guests were in the Royal Box. There is a tiny dining room off the box, and footmen were on duty to serve the meal (transported from the Palace) during the two intervals. The Princess was entertaining a party of six, and the staff had laid up the table and lit the candelabra, and it all looked rather good, with the light glittering off the white linen, the Palace silver, and crystal.

In the party was a rather young and impressionable girl, who said as they came into the small dining area, "Oh, ma'am, what an enchanting room!" "I'm so glad you like it," drawled the Princess. "It used to be my great-grandfather's loo."

And, actually, it was. The room had once been called the King's Smoking Room—a euphemism for a rather elaborate lavatory—and has now been turned into a dining room.

Princess Margaret has a sort of 1920s blasé attitude to life. One incident completely sums up her reactions to situations. It was some years ago, when Sandringham was being restored and the family were "mucking in"—staying in various houses scattered about the estate. The Queen Mother had moved into Hillingdon House, which was owned by Lady Fermoy, Princess Diana's grandmother. Princess Margaret, who says she cannot afford a country home and does not own one, moved in with her mother, taking her children, Sarah and David, plus their nanny.

The Queen Mother then had a footman who liked a drink. One day the Royals had all been out, and they returned to Hillingdon House to find that Nanny Sumner had locked herself in the nursery with the children. And the din they heard as they came into the house was the footman trying to break down the nursery door. He disappeared rather fast as he heard Princess Margaret coming up the stairs.

"Is everything all right, Nanny?" she called.

Nanny unlocked the door, and her red, furious face appeared around the jamb.

"No, it is not, Your Royal Highness," she spluttered, and launched into the tale of the footman's perfidies. The Princess listened sympathetically, clucked her dismay at such goings-on, and then went downstairs to get herself a drink. As a page was fixing her favorite whisky and water, she told him the story.

"I wouldn't mind," she concluded, "but he knows that Nanny only likes sherry. He was trying to force a Scotch on her."

Later, however, he was sacked.

Nanny Sumner was, and still is, a marvelous woman. She brought up Princess Margaret's children by Lord Snowdon beautifully, and was a pillar of strength in a rocky household. She never faltered day or night, and the children have turned out charmingly; they know how to share and have delightful manners.

She wasn't particularly liked by the other staff because when she went to stay in the Queen's homes, she was extremely fussy. She and the Royal Nanny, Mabel Anderson, couldn't stand each other. When they met it was very much "Good morning, Nanny Sumner," and "Good morning, Miss Anderson," with Miss Anderson pulling rank. They were always extremely formal with each other. But the real bone of contention was that Nanny Anderson, as the Palace nanny, had the most perfectly run nursery and constant service herself. Nanny Sumner was not going to play second fiddle, and demanded exactly the same high standard.

But the children adored her. When they were too grown-up for a nanny and she left to live in Kennington, on the Duchy of Cornwall estate, they bought her a color television set as a farewell present.

Nanny Sumner was another of the Royal service women who couldn't tolerate her mistress's men. She could not stand Lord Snowdon at any price. He in turn could not stand her, and they never spoke. Rather a pity, really, as they are both nice people. The happiest day in that household, as far as staff were concerned, was when Lord Snowdon moved out and the women had their Princess to themselves again. Miss Matheson, the Princess's dresser, was jubilant. So was the house manageress, a lady called Greenhill. Lord Snowdon had always referred to her as Green Shield Stamps.

The consensus was, as Nanny Sumner said to me, that "Now life will get back to normal," which was pretty much what Miss Matheson felt, too.

It was sad, really, because Lord Snowdon is a charmer, but his problem was being married to a Princess. He was far too independent to lead the Royal life. He wanted to work, and he did. Now he is one of the most successful photographers in Britain—if not the world. Mind you, his connections with Royalty didn't do him any harm in the early days of his career. He once fell afoul of the Duke of Edinburgh when they were all out shooting at Windsor. Lord Snowdon, usually a good shot (though he has since given up shooting), was having a bad day and missing quite a few birds. Finally the Duke turned around and snapped at him, "For God's sake, Tony, why don't you shoot with your bloody camera? You might do better."

In spite of all the quarrels and the final break, the marriage did produce two charming children. The Queen is enormously fond of Lady Sarah Armstrong-Jones, and seemed to take her under her wing to a great extent. She would take Lady Sarah to Windsor for the weekend with her when Lady Sarah's mother was away. It was the Queen who taught the little girl to ride when she was old enough and generally helped give her a secure background. I used to wonder if perhaps the Queen would have liked another daughter.

Princess Margaret is the odd one out of the family. She is the only Royal who never sends Christmas cards. In a family mad about dogs, she doesn't like them much. She did have a King Charles spaniel called Rolly, but he was a publicity dog, only produced for photographers. At Windsor, at Christmas, Princess Margaret is always the first to get bored with the family scene, and have dinner in bed instead of with her vast crowd of relatives. She is not "cozy" like the rest of them.

Old James Frost, a butler who served the Royal Family for many years, was once working for the Queen Mother at Royal Lodge, when Princess Margaret was staying there in her absence. The Queen Mother had left James a gift, telling the Princess to present it to him on her behalf. Christmas came and went. James knew the big wooden box in the corner was for him, but nothing happened.

Then one morning the Princess came back from riding. Still in her jodhpurs, she called him in and said, "James, this is from Her Majesty, wishing you a happy Christmas." Then she gave the box a booted kick, and added, "I don't know what's in it, but it weighs a ton."

Princess Margaret's near neighbor at Kensington Palace is Princess Michael, the new and also rather controversial member of the Royal Family. Princess Margaret doesn't care for her much. No one in the family does. The Queen is reputed to have said of her, "She's much too Royal for us." This may be true, or it may be a variation of something Her Majesty *did* say about Marion Stein, the Earl of Harewood's first wife. The Countess of Harewood was musical, and very highbrow and grand. The Queen actually did complain one day, "That woman always makes me feel like the cook."

And Prince Charles, when taking Anna Wallace (one of his girlfriends) around Windsor during Ascot Week, just before he met Lady Diana, told her behind his hand, "Don't bother to curtsy to Princess Michael."

Certainly Princess Michael, married to the younger son of the Kent family, is grand. But grand on a shoestring. Being the second son, her husband receives no money from the Civil List. The Princess, who married Prince Michael in 1978, is seen today on every balcony, at every Trooping of the Color, at every Royal ceremony she can wheel herself into. She is always beautifully dressed, looking straight ahead, smiling and towering over Princess Margaret and the Queen. Only Princess Diana matches her for height.

At first Princess Michael believed that if she worked hard enough, eventually she and Prince Michael would be put on the Civil List, but the rules are the rules and that will never happen. As it is, there is a lot of to-ing and fro-ing between Kensington Palace and Christie's—the auctioneers—where they quietly sell off some of the more obscure pieces of the family heritage.

The marriage did cause some consternation in the Royal Family, as Princess Michael, born Baroness Marie-Christine von Reibnitz, had previously been married for three years to a London socialite, one Tom Troubridge. She is also a Roman Catholic, which the Queen, as head of the Church of England, found a little embarrassing. After Prince Michael met and fell in love with her, he went to see Lord Mountbatten at Broadlands to ask what they should do. Live in sin or marry?

"Which is worse for the Monarch?" Lord Mountbatten said. "Living in sin, of course. Far better to marry."

His strong advice was that Marie-Christine give up her religion, but she simply would not do this. They could not be married in Britain, because Royalty cannot marry a Catholic in a Church of England church. And Prince Michael, who was in the line of succession to the throne, could hardly marry in a Catholic church in England.

In the end, the Queen gave her consent to the marriage, which took place in a registrar's office in Vienna. The new Princess was bitterly disappointed when the Pope refused the dispensation that would have allowed them to be married in a Catholic ceremony.

By marrying Marie-Christine, Prince Michael lost his right of succession to the throne, but in order that children of the marriage should remain on the list of succession, the Princess did agree that her children should be brought up in the Church of England faith. This was something that had made for a sticking point with the Vatican, and caused it to refuse the dispensation. The Catholic Church finally softened and permitted the couple to have their marriage validated by Archbishop Bruno Heim, the Pope's ambassador, in Westminster Cathedral in London. It took five years.

Princess Michael has made herself popular with the British public, though the Royals are not too certain about her. Princess Margaret refuses to speak to her while she retains her Catholic religion. Princess Margaret was outraged by the marriage—perhaps painfully reminded that she could not marry the man she had first loved because he had been divorced. Her feelings obviously run through her family. Her son, Lord Lindley, had to make a public apology for saying that as a Christmas present to his worst enemy, he would give "dinner with Princess Michael."

Marie-Christine, as she is called in the family, has the smart taste that the Royals, with their love for anything "cozy," distrust. She didn't actually help the situation when she was put in the Edward III Tower at Windsor for Christmas. Each Royal branch—the Waleses, the Kents, the Gloucesters—is assigned its own tower. As old as it sounds, the Edward III Tower is the most modern, having been done up in the sixties by a series of top British designers. The Queen felt that as an example of her modern reign, she would like to have a modern tower. Princess Michael, who is by profession an interior decorator, took one look around her in horror.

"This decor is awful," she said to the page who was showing her her rooms.

The page trotted back to the Queen's tower, where she asked if everyone was all right.

"Yes, Your Majesty," he said, "but Princess Michael doesn't seem to like her rooms."

"Really?" said the Queen, her wedding ring whizzing around a bit.

That evening, at drinks before dinner, when the Queen greeted all her guests, relations, and in-laws, she came to Princess Michael and said, "Welcome for Christmas. Is everything all right?"

"Oh, yes, ma'am," said Princess Michael, curtsying deeply.

"So pleased," said the Queen silkily, and moved on. The next year she put Princess Michael back in the same tower.

To be fair, Princess Michael has made her apartment at Kensington Palace quite superb, for she does have marvelous taste. But there was a lot of hilarity backstairs about the story of the roof terrace. Just after the Prince of Wales married and moved into Kensington Palace, the Department of the Environment constructed the most splendid roof terrace for his apartment. It is large, sunny, and runs the full length of two apartments, with a greenhouse in the center, a barbecue, and lots of garden furniture. It is also completely private—not overlooked by another building at all.

Princess Michael, the Waleses' next-door neighbor, watched this going up, and wanted one, too. She sent for the man in charge of maintenance at Kensington Palace and put in a request, but he turned her down flat, saying it would cost too much. He also explained that her roof was constructed differently, and it wouldn't be possible.

Not to be defeated, she invited Michael Heseltine, the Secretary for the Environment, to dinner and tackled him over the pudding.

"Wouldn't it be lovely," she said, "for the children to have some fresh air in London?" She did not mention the small garden that goes with the apartment. Caught in difficult circumstances, Michael Heseltine agreed it would indeed be lovely for the children to have some fresh air, and yes, she could have a balcony terrace.

Unfortunately, it doesn't quite match up to the Waleses'.

For a start, as it clings to the side of the building, it is over-looked by the Prince of Wales's staff and the Waleses themselves, if they feel like hanging out of the bedroom windows. It is very small and laid out with phony grass, with room for just two chairs. Princess Michael's heart must burn when she thinks of the splendid roof garden above her head where Princess Diana sunbathes.

There are delusions of grandeur. She suggested to an American newspaper group that they should have Prince Michael on their board. In turn, the proprietors invited the Prince and Princess to the Kentucky Derby. Princess Michael accepted with alacrity, but then said she wanted to bring an entourage with her, including ladies-in-waiting and a hairdresser. Her hosts balked at this. She had to cut the numbers.

She has quite a small staff, and they have mostly come from the Palace for the promotion. She had a butler, Ian Armstrong, who was a second valet to Prince Charles when I worked for him. She got on quite well with him, though they quarreled a bit in a rather gentle way. She is not entitled to a policeman, by the Royal rules, but she always has one in tow. They don't have a Royal-type car, but drive a splendid green Jaguar, which Ian used to chauffeur.

"We were just approaching the V and A," he once said, "when she suddenly said from the back seat, 'Ian, put on all the car lights so people can see me.'

"Well, there wasn't anyone about, and it looked silly in a Jaguar, arriving with the map light on, the overhead light on —any old lights I could find. It's not that sort of car. I just got out and let *her* out as quickly as possible." In the end, Ian got fed up with all the pretensions and left. "Not like working for Prince Charles," he said.

Martin Bubb left the Palace to replace him as her butler just about the time she bought a small country house in Gloucestershire. One weekend they all went down to unpack and sort things out.

She said to Martin, "Do you like painting?" He was in the middle of trying to get things organized, but he stopped and thought about the question for a moment, understanding her to mean painting in oils or watercolors.

"I'd like to try," he said, "but don't know if I'd be any good."

"What are you doing next week?" she then asked, and before he could answer, added, "Perhaps you could have a go at painting the stables." She went back to London, and there he was, slapping white paint on stable walls. Not surprisingly, he, too, left soon after.

Prince Michael, her husband, is pleasant enough: a good-looking, bearded young man who looks remarkably like his grandfather, George V. Without Marie-Christine doing her Royal act, it's unlikely that anyone in Britain would have given him a second thought. He was just another soldier who happened to be a Royal Duke.

He does have more charisma than his cousin, the Duke of Gloucester. Coming unexpectedly to the title, this Duke was also a second son until his brother was killed in an air crash. Because he is now the first son, he is on the Civil List; so it has become his fate and that of his wife, Princess Birgitte, to undertake a certain amount of public duties. Neither of them really has the temperament, though they are charming and kind. So, not surprisingly, they are barely known by the British public, which I suspect suits them very well.

They were on a public engagement in Gloucestershire, and it just so happened that an ex-footman from the Duke's late father's staff was in town. He decided to give them a bit of support. So he and his sister went along to Gloucester Town Hall, where the Duke and Duchess were having lunch with the mayor.

"We were going to cheer a bit when they came out," he told me, "but when we got there we were surprised and pleased to see some crash barriers and quite a good crowd on the pavement opposite the entrance to the town hall. I was thinking that he must be more popular than I'd thought, when a bus came along—and everyone in sight got on it.

"We'd been standing in a bus queue! When the Duke and Duchess came out, only my sister and I were left."

The gentle Princess Birgitte lives with her mother-in-law, Princess Alice of Gloucester, in yet another grace-and-favor apartment in Kensington Palace. They seem to get on fine.

Princess Alexandra is the only Kent female Royal. Her older brother, Eddie, is the Duke, and her younger brother is Prince Michael of Kent. Alexandra is undoubtedly the most popular Royal with Royals—she is an absolute darling. She lives with her husband, Angus Ogilvy, and their children at St. James's Palace, next door to the Queen Mother. The Duke and Duchess of Kent, Alexandra's brother and sister-in-law, live there too.

The Princess is deeply loved by her staff, though as she is not one of the richer Royals, her household is small. She solves one of her servant problems by not taking on a chef. Instead she employs four women who cook on a monthly rota, so that they each work for a week at a time.

This works out very well, except for one funny habit of the Princess. She gets hungry in the night, and she is always creeping down to the fridge for a midnight snack. Her duty cook will come in and find a perfect quiche, all ready for a luncheon party that day, that has a neat slice out of it.

"I'm sorry," the Princess says. "But it looked so *good*." Her cooks spend their lives trying to cover holes in foods with watercress or salad.

Her husband, businessman Angus Ogilvy, has his funny little ways, too. He had a habit of coming home after lunch and settling down on the bed for a nap while staring up at the ceiling. By the time he was fully awake again, he would decide he didn't care for the color of the ceiling and have it repainted. It used to drive the man from the Department of the Environment mad.

The only Royal without a town house is Princess Anne.

She still stays at Buckingham Palace when she is in London. She runs the most informal of all the Royal houses at her home, Gatcombe Park, which her husband manages as a thriving farm. Richard, her butler, complained that everyone came into the house in jeans and jodhpurs, and that it was "open house" for the grooms, farmhands, and anyone else who felt like popping in. Richard is a butler of the old school, trained at the Palace, loving beautiful things and what he calls "things done properly."

He believes that the back stairs, the kitchen, and the pantry belong to the Staff. The drawing room and the dining room are the Royals'. And Royals have no place in his part of the establishment. It is, he says, tidier and easier for everyone to keep a division.

Normally this would be true of all the Royal Family. Those at Buckingham Palace or Sandringham who work with the horses or dogs would never come into the Palace or house itself, except perhaps the married ones for their meals. Everyone else stays in his own quarters.

But Gatcombe is completely informal. There are no footmen, no large live-in staff. Daily cleaners come in from the village. It could be the residence of any gentleman farmer, rather than that of the daughter of the Queen. I always remember, just before Prince Charles had his own country house, Highgrove, redecorated, when he decided to give a Christmas tea party there for little Peter, Princess Anne's son. The Parker Bowleses' son, Tom, came, and some local children. Mabel Anderson, the Prince's old nanny, was working for the Princess at the time, and she came over to supervise the party.

It was great fun, with a magician from London and lots of party games. Palace staff came down to do the work, paid for by Prince Charles—but more than that, Nanny Anderson was in her element. "Things," she said, echoing Richard, "were being done properly."

At Princess Anne's house Nanny had to carry her own

food up to her room and clean the nursery. Having spent so many years at the Palace, with two nursery footmen and nursery maids on tap, she really found it very hard to adjust.

She had always loved Prince Charles, and had he married first and to someone different, she would probably still be in Royal service. But Princess Diana wanted a less traditional nanny for Prince William. As it happened, Mabel went to Gatcombe because Princess Anne produced the first Royal grandchild, but she has now left and works in a more formal house, where there are footmen and proper service.

But even at Highgrove that day she was beginning to look out of place. Master Peter wanted crisps and sausages and Twiglets for his party. Mabel, in her dark dress, was sighing for the days of Swiss Rolls and a trifle. There wasn't a jam penny in sight.

Gatcombe was not for her, with a mistress who always wore jeans, and with girl grooms all over the place, frequently running amok. One, who had been out with Prince Edward, managed to crash Captain Phillips's car. She had borrowed it from Gatcombe to come up to London to see the Prince. It was all rather unfortunate. The car she hit was a fine antique one that had been lovingly restored; its owner was towing it on a trailer, late at night, believing this would be the safest time to move it. But the girl groom drove into him and wrote it off.

At the time there was a lot of press speculation as to whether a girl groom was involved with Captain Phillips. They were nearly right, but they got the name wrong. It was Prince Edward.

Actually, the Princess and her husband get along very well. It is true he is not the Brain of Britain, and his nickname, "Fog," has a ring of truth. But he is likable and easygoing. And he tries.

Princess Anne remarked one day how lovely it would be to have fresh eggs. Real new-laid ones. Captain Phillips, wanting to please his wife, went out and bought some birds.

He let them roam loose around the farm so that the eggs would be truly free range, and then waited.

He had to wait a very long time. He'd bought bantams. Which perhaps explains why there are those who say his time at agricultural college did not take.

Princess Anne has the brains and she does not suffer fools gladly. She might be informal at home on the farm, but she still loves the trappings of Royalty. On her engagements, she always looks the part, with the hat, the brooch, and the neatly cut coat.

I remember once at Balmoral when they were all going off to the Highland Gathering at Braemar and were congregating in the hall. Princess Anne was late and rushed down the stairs, apologizing. The Queen gave her a hard look.

"Why aren't you wearing a hat?" she asked.

"Do I have to?" said the Princess.

"You must," the Queen said firmly. "You know you look like a sheepdog if you don't."

I too was in the hall, and had to turn away to hide a giggle.

I think perhaps that since the Royal wedding there has been a little jealousy between Anne and Diana. Suddenly Anne never stops working; yet only a few years back there were constant taxpayer questions and grumbles about what she did to earn her Civil List money. She certainly earns it today. She has done the most amazing and sterling work for the Save the Children Fund, operating in countries and conditions that no Royal would have dreamed of tackling before her.

Also, she seems to have got her own house in order. She used to go through private secretaries like a dose of salts, but she has had a new man since December 1982 and they seem to get on well. Apart from her Save the Children Fund work, she is doing a lot of official engagements, usually by helicopter from Benson RAF Station in Oxfordshire. Her ladies-in-waiting drive down from London to join her. She is acting like a bona fide Royal.

A PRIDE OF PRINCESSES

I think Anne is determined to keep her position in the Royal hierarchy. For example, the Royal Regiment has just celebrated three hundred years. They haven't had a Colonel-in-Chief since the Princess Royal died. The men were rather hoping to get the glamorous Princess Diana, but Princess Anne got the job.

Personally, I believe her popularity will grow. The Queen has a long time to go. Princess Diana will eventually get bogged down with children; Princess Anne could become the much-loved character of the family. In fact just recently, at the end of 1983, she did actually come out above Princess Diana in a popularity poll. And what Anne has is staying power.

Her husband, Captain Mark Phillips, is from the landed aristocracy, a group that considers itself quite as good as nobility. I suspect that this may be the reason he turned down a title at the time of his marriage, in 1973. He had Anne's support in this decision, and she quite likes being known as The Princess Anne, Mrs. Mark Phillips.

But the effect of his not taking a title is that the Queen's two oldest grandchildren are simply Peter and Zara Phillips. This leaves them and the Ogilvy children, whose father made the same decision to reject a title, as the only plain-styled Royal children. No doubt, living in the world they do, the girls will probably marry titles one of these days. But the boys will remain plain Mister unless the Queen decides to ennoble them.

Titled or not, Princess Anne's little Peter is definitely a gentleman. One day at a polo match he came up and gave me his last piece of candy.

How many kids would do that?

Chapter Eight

ROYAL PENNY-PINCHING AND FINANCES

I MUST SAY THAT IN ALL MY YEARS OF ROYAL SERVICE, I DID sometimes wonder if the Queen really is the richest woman in the world, or if it is all a myth.

The entire family never stops moaning, "I can't afford it." And there is nothing they will not do to save a bob or two if the money comes from their own private incomes.

Prince Charles, for example, cannot bear to waste toothpaste. He has a little silver gadget that rolls the toothpaste up from the end, making sure none is missed. The gadget is inscribed with his Prince of Wales feather emblem, and he uses it to squeeze out the last little bit of his Macleans from the container.

Definitely a present for the man who has everything and intends to keep it.

Yet life at Buckingham Palace or any of the other Royal

homes is nowhere near as luxurious as it is at any first-class hotel. Take the Royal bed linen. The sheets for the five days the family are at the Palace are turned top to tail, and under to over; they are most certainly not changed daily.

The staff bed linen is "topped and tailed" once a week.

The Palace laundry used to be washed on the premises until it was decided that this was not cost-effective. Now the Queen's sheets and pillowcases are sent to the Sycamore Laundry in Clapham (a none too salubrious area of London), where the Royals are given a special rate. Indeed, I believe that they hold shares in the enterprise. And certainly the Sycamore Laundry has the Royal Warrant.

Tea towels and similar items are still washed at the Palace. A large industrial machine is kept in the basement. Table linen is not too much of a problem at Windsor or Buckingham Palace, as food is served on polished wood and a tablecloth is not necessary. They do use beautiful ones in their own homes—Balmoral and Sandringham. Most of the linen dates back to the time of Queen Victoria. The damask table napkins, embossed with her crest, are still in service, but they are so large that they are used as tray cloths these days.

Should any of the table linen show signs of wear, the linen room lady is put to carefully repairing and darning them. The Royals never throw anything away if it is salvageable, but in fairness, most of the time this is because they like to say "This was great-granny's," though the fact that they would then not have to buy new ones is also a consideration. It's fifty-fifty between the cost of replacement and continuing tradition.

The Queen's pet penny-pinching is that she can't bear to waste electricity. One day, when I was a young footman on duty at Balmoral, I was sitting outside the tower door, which is one of the entrances and which leads into the office of the Queen's Private Secretary.

Since it was a typical Scottish summer day, with a midday

darkness, the other young footman on duty and I had turned on the three bare electric lights that hang in the entrance.

The Queen returned from a walk, corgis running behind and in front. She came in the door, made a small "huh," and, without saying a word, ran her hand over the switch that controlled all three lights, then strode on, leaving us in the gloom.

We didn't dare turn them back on again even when she was out of sight.

She has much the same attitude about central heating. At the Palace and Windsor Castle, where the heating bills come out of the money paid to her by the State, the radiators blaze away. However, in her own homes, Balmoral and Sandringham, it's a case of "If you're cold, put on a pullover."

Another Royal economy is on petrol. Balmoral is roughly an hour's drive from the nearest station, Aberdeen. In the old days, staff used to be ferried back and forth by car. We could swap our days off with one another and roughly make up our own working rota. This meant that cars were going to Aberdeen station all the time. Now the staff rota has to be strictly upheld so that all changeovers take place at the same time and there is only one trip to the station, with a car carrying several people. And indeed, staff traveling expenses are gone through with a fine-tooth comb. In this way, working for Royalty is like working for any money-conscious business. The ordinary Staff most certainly do not get to travel first class. As Prince Charles's valet, happily I did.

And like any well-run company, the Royals do look for discounts where they can find them, yet curiously they always pay the full price for all the wines and spirits that they buy. It costs the Queen a great deal less to give a cocktail party in one of her Embassies than it does in Buckingham Palace. We used to joke that perhaps it was because they paid the full price that they were so careful with the liquor.

ROYAL PENNY-PINCHING AND FINANCES

I have known occasions when they would make a bottle of wine go around eight.

Though there are exceptions, it's not easy to get a little intoxicated when formally dining with the Queen or Prince Charles. The same cannot be said for either the Queen Mother, who is a most generous hostess, or Princess Margaret, who gives splendid staff parties. These only last for two hours, are carefully planned, extremely generous, and enjoyed by all. In no way are they great wing-dings, but they are perfect parties and all the staff consider it a great honor to be asked.

The Royals don't waste food, Prince Charles especially. His girlfriends used to be amazed at the odd bits of leftovers he would concoct into a meal when we were away from the Palace, usually with me having to make it look interesting and appetizing. I remember Princess Diana's bewilderment when she was first served one of his pot-luck, left-over repasts. And, honestly, who could blame her.

When Prince Philip takes his staff out for Christmas lunch he will likely go to a hotel, perhaps the Savoy or the Dorchester. But he takes along his own wine, from Buckingham Palace. One of the chauffeurs delivers it to the hotel the day before the gathering.

"Wine is far too expensive in restaurants," he says and, since he is who he is, the restaurants let him get away with it. Prince Charles, who always took his staff out at Christmas to a different place each year, certainly does not do the same.

Princess Alice, the Dowager Duchess of Gloucester, was born the daughter of the Duke of Buccleuch. He was one of the richest landowners in Britain; but her husband, the Duke, who died in 1974, was one of the poorer relations, and had to be supported to some degree by his brother, King George VI. One Christmas, the Dowager Duchess gave each of her staff a chrysanthemum plant in a pot, but asked, "Would you please be kind enough to give the pot back to the gardener when the plant dies?"

Another year she called the old Duke's valet to give him his Christmas present. They were staying as the Queen's guests in the Lancaster Tower at Windsor, surrounded by the most incredible art treasures and fine furniture. The Duchess, going through the usual Christmas ritual, said graciously, "There is a small present on the table for you with our best wishes." Small it was. A blue handkerchief and a brown one, unwrapped.

"Choose which you like," she said, "and leave the other."

When the present Duke married, Prince Charles told me to find out what they would like for a wedding present. I checked it out with the young Duke's private secretary, and came back to see the Prince.

"They would like monogrammed silver table-mats, sir," I told him.

"Fine," he said. So I ordered them, and when a dozen arrived at the Palace, plus the bill, the Prince exploded.

"Christ! What's this?" he demanded, shaking the bill at me.

"The Duke and Duchess of Gloucester's wedding present, sir," I said. "You did authorize it."

He looked at the bill again, and shook his head.

"Well, at that price," he finally said, "just give them two for the time being."

And he's been giving them two every Christmas since. They'll be able to hold a dinner party soon!

When Princess Anne and Mark Phillips married, their cousin-by-marriage David Hicks had no difficulty in deciding what to give them for a wedding present. He is a well-known British interior designer whose connection with Royalty has done him no harm at all. His present: He did a room for them.

He did the same for Prince Charles on the latter's twenty-first birthday. But did he supply any of the furniture, carpets, curtains, or wallpaper? He did not! He merely gave them the benefit of his advice. And not quite the best advice, as it turned out. The fabric he chose for Prince Charles's sitting room was blue; it faded. The curtains shrank when they were cleaned; now they do not meet.

But then, the curtains in the Queen's dining room might meet if they were pulled, but they would certainly fall to pieces. Happily, they are never closed. But the yellowy damask, embossed with a traditional design, has been hanging so long that it is only held together by the lining.

There is a great reluctance to part with anything. On the second floor of the Palace, there are cupboards and cupboards full of clothes, dating back years. The stories that the Queen gives her old clothes to charity are not true. They are all stored. Fortunately, they have a lot of rooms for storage. Also on the second floor are a collection of tin trunks holding uniforms dating back to the time of Edward VII. In those days members of British Royalty were given honorary ranks in European services and acquired the uniforms of Field Marshals, Colonels, and so on, to go with the ranks. The Imperial War Museum would love to get their hands on the contents of those trunks, but they are kept securely at the Palace.

The clothes of King George VI, the Queen's father, are still there. Various valets over the years have thought of clearing them out, but it would require permission from the Queen Mother, and no one dares suggest it.

All these clothes—and particularly the Queen's robes of State—are the responsibility of any valet who retires in service. In return for his pension and for his grace-and-favor residence, he is expected to keep an eye on the Royal wardrobes and robes—a two-day-a-week task. At present this is the job of the Duke of Edinburgh's retired valet, James McDonald, who cares for the robes of State—a long red cloak for the Queen, a black one for the Duke—most expertly. These garments are not hung or packed flat, but are rolled up like sausages. And they are expected to last an entire reign, as they are only worn at the yearly State opening of Parliament.

As we are much the same size, I used to wear Prince Charles's clothes for portrait painters when he had no time to sit, and the Duke of Edinburgh also had a valet who was exactly his size and would go to the tailor for fittings. But there was never any question of a Royal hand-me-down, since neither Prince Charles nor his father ever seems to actually wear out a suit. And why should they, as their clothing is of the finest quality and is well taken care of.

The children's clothes, on the other hand, are passed on to the next little Royal in the lineup. Again, these never wear out, and the Royal style is so traditional that nursery garments never go out of fashion. Even if they did, it might worry Princess Diana, but it certainly would not worry the immediate Royal family. None of them is deeply into what is fashionable.

Sometimes the Royals' reluctance to part with money costs them dearly. When Queen Victoria bought Balmoral as a present for her husband, Prince Albert, she was offered a great deal of the surrounding land, but she chose to lease this to expand the shooting.

In the mid-seventies the lease ran out, and the land reverted to its owner, the Laird of Invercauld. He owns most of the acreage between Braemar and Ballater, the two villages on the Balmoral estate. He promptly let off the land again, much more profitably, to some wealthy Arabs, and now also charges them for the pleasure of shooting the grouse.

The Prince and the Duke, ever conscious of their manly image, walk everywhere. And so do their guests. The only ones who get away with riding while out shooting are those who are not in top shape, like the aforementioned Denis Dawnay, who has a heart condition and gets to sit in the Land-Rover.

ROYAL PENNY-PINCHING AND FINANCES

Arabs and foreign visitors will not walk anywhere when they can ride. The Royals are furious, because the new lessees have built roads of rough pebble-dash across the shoot, and these have made ugly scars on the hillside.

As the Prince and the Duke trudge over the brow of the hill from Balmoral, these scars suddenly come into view.

"Bloody roads!" the Duke is always raging. "Don't they realize that if the birds are flying this way and they see roads they take fright and fly back in the opposite direction?" According to him, the paler strip of color against the dark moorland deflects the birds' flight, ruining the shooting.

The Royals have now had to buy other land from Viscount Cowdrey, a forty-minute drive away on a tarmac road, right across country and nowhere near the house. They hate having roads near Balmoral, feeling the entire area should be for their use alone. But, of course, Scotland is always swarming with tourists, and even Royalty can't keep them away.

To their intense irritation, holiday-makers took little notice of PRIVATE PROPERTY or KEEP OFF signs. Then the Duke had a brilliant idea. He erected new signs, and these proved to be exceedingly effective. They read: BEWARE OF ADDERS.

IN SOME SITUATIONS, THE ROYAL FAMILY COULD BE SHARPER or better advised. A government scheme for turning sections of big estates into parkland for the public, in return for tax concessions, attracted Prince Philip. He gave away a few bogs and a gravel pit—some of the less attractive areas of Sandringham.

They do seem to let their property deteriorate considerably before they do anything about it, generally because they are badly advised. There is a lovely old house called Frogmore in the grounds at Windsor, where Queen Victoria is buried.

During fashion: the Princess of Wales wearing a dinner suit at a pop concert, accompanied by her husband. (Rex Features Ltd.)

Princess Diana: looking stunning during her pregnancy in July 1984. (Rex Features Ltd.)

The Prince and Princess of Wales leaving St. Mary's Hospital after the birth of Prince Henry. (Rex Features Ltd.)

Prince William boarding one of the Royal Aircraft with his father. (© Lionel Cherruault)

Prince William with his mother and father in August 1984. (© Lionel Cherruault)

Prince William going for a stroll with Nanny Barnes in Regent's Park.
(Mauro Carraro, Rex Features Ltd.)

Highgrove, the country residence of the Prince and Princess of Wales.
(Rex Features Ltd.)

*Britannia, the Royal Yacht, the Queen's floating palace, shown here in California.
(Rex Features Ltd.)*

The staff and crew on the Brittania, *with Queen Elizabeth and the Duke of
Edinburgh seated in the center. This photo was taken on the Royal Yacht in 1970
during my first tour with the Queen. I'm seated on the deck, in front of Princess
Anne, who's on the left of her mother.*

*Lord Mountbatten and his grandnephew Prince Charles in Nepal. The two were
always very close. A man of enormous charm and equally enormous vanity, Lord
Mountbatten loved the trappings of position. He often encouraged Prince Charles to wear
more medals and decorations by saying, "If you've got it, wear it." (Rex Features Ltd.)*

The Queen Mother with her eldest grandson on her birthday. (Mauro Carraro, Rex Features Ltd.)

The Queen Mother and Princess Diana at Ascot. On the back of the carriage are the footmen in scarlet. The one on the left, however, is really a Royal bodyguard. (© Lionel Cherruault)

Princess Margaret and Prince Andrew disembarking from the Royal Yacht.
(© Lionel Cherruault)

Prince Andrew at the Chester shoot.
(© Lionel Cherruault)

Prince Edward. (© Lionel Cherruault)

Princess Anne in the country. (Rex Features Ltd.)

Princess Michael of Kent, one of the newest and grandest members of the Royal Family. (Rex Features Ltd.)

The Queen had been planning to give this to Prince Charles as a country house, long before he bought Highgrove.

"It's not on, though," the Prince said to me one day. "We've discovered it will cost a million pounds to put it back in order."

Each Royal house is overseen by the Estate Office. There is a paid man on the premises who is supposed to make sure that the fabric of the house is in good condition, that the furniture is repaired, and the rooms redecorated on a rotating basis.

In order to please the Royals, the man at Sandringham used to cut costs like crazy. The Palace was delighted, thinking that the house was being run very cheaply. That went on for so long that the place fell into a state of such bad repair that they had to move out for three years while it was put right. And the repairs cost £400,000 out of the Queen's own Privy Purse.

If the Royals are more hard-up than seems likely, a lot of the blame lies squarely on the shoulders of the late Duke of Windsor. He cost them a fortune. After his marriage to Wallis Simpson in 1937, it became clear that the Royals would never relent and let her become Her Royal Highness. He retaliated by threatening to sell both Balmoral and Sandringham.

King George VI was forced to buy them back from him over the years. The price the family had to pay is said to be one million pounds for both houses—a vast sum in 1937. But it did not stop there. The Duke demanded a pension of £60,000 a year for life. It certainly kept the Duke and his divorcée Duchess living in the style to which he was accustomed. And this is yet another reason why the Queen Mother was not too keen on the Windsors. The intention of Queen Victoria was that the two houses would automatically be inherited by the Monarch.

At Balmoral, the Royals saved a fortune in staff bills. In the 1960s, when I first started work at the Palace, the army

ROYAL PENNY-PINCHING AND FINANCES

used to come there every summer and take over a lot of the work. They would do the kitchen and baggage portering, bring in ice, and deal with the sorts of jobs that no one else particularly wanted to do.

It was about that time that Sir Philip Moore, the Queen's Private Secretary, joined her Household. When he first came to Balmoral he was horrified to find that the army was being used in this way. There was a socialist government at the time, and he could foresee the criticism that must inevitably come if the story got out. He stopped the practice immediately.

Not that any of the soldiers really minded at the time; they enjoyed the change. And so did the housemaids! And the occasional footman . . .

The other chore that the Royals used the army for, on the cheap, was beating. Running a shoot is an expensive business, and it was costing about £7 a day to employ a beater. At a Royal shoot there are generally about thirty of them. The official story was that the army were doing the work as an exercise to keep fit. So half a regiment would come beating and walk for miles. The loyalty to the Queen in the army is quite amazing; one word from her and they'd have walked until they dropped.

The officers adored it. They didn't do any walking, and got invited to dinner.

The excuse that it was "exercise" went on for a long time. The truth was that it was cheap labor. Even today the army move the Court three times a year—at Christmas, April, and Ascot Week in June. No mean task—and it's all done for free.

All the Royal poverty talk has to be taken with a pinch of salt, when one knows that over 75% of the expenses incurred in running the Monarchy are paid by Departmental Appropriations—in other words, the British taxpayer.

These Departmental Appropriations do not include the

Civil List, which, in 1983, paid out £4,311,983 to the Queen and her family. The Royal Yacht, the Queen's Flight of three rather ancient Andovers (soon to be replaced), the two helicopters (costing £3,000,000 a year), the Royal Train, and the actual upkeep of all the palaces and houses are paid for by different appropriations from the national budget, which amount to a sum in the region of £28,000,000.

Prince Philip's office staff are paid for by him, but he borrows heavily from the Queen's staff, leaving his £179,300 from the Civil List virtually untouched. And he is in the fortunate position of not having to pay income tax on this money. He has two valets, both from the army, so the main part of their salaries will be paid by the defense ministry. He has a treasurer, a clerk to the office, four or five female secretaries, and two pages—which last, as we have already said, are the most underemployed people at the Palace.

The Queen's own share of the Civil List came, roughly speaking, to £3,610,000 in 1983. And just as a matter of interest, this is where the money went:

Wages	£2,523,000
Food	255,000
4 Garden parties	140,000
Horses	85,000
Household goods	75,000
Cellars	70,000
Cars	55,000
Laundry	45,000
Flowers	40,000
Sandringham and Balmoral expenses	40,000
Liveries	30,000
Allowances and gratuities	30,000
Staff travel	30,000
Official presents	30,000
Windsor gardens	25,000
Chapels	25,000
Subscriptions, trophies, medals	20,000

Rent and rates	10,000
Newspapers	8,000
Windsor library	5,000
Sundries	69,000
Total	£3,610,000

The remainder of the Civil List money (about £760,000) is paid out to relatives. Again in 1983, this is the way it was distributed:

Queen Elizabeth, the Queen Mother	£321,500
The Duke of Edinburgh	179,300
Princess Anne	111,700
Prince Andrew	20,000
Prince Edward	20,000
Princess Margaret	108,700

The Queen pays four of the Royal relatives an allowance from her own slice of the Civil List:

Princess Alice	£44,000
The Duke of Gloucester	86,000
The Duke of Kent	118,000
Princess Alexandra	112,700

The Queen is paid this money in one lump sum in April, on Budget Day. She then doles it out to the relatives, bit by bit, throughout the twelve months of the year. Imagine how much interest this huge sum must make for her, wisely invested in short-term loans. And the interest accrued stays in the family. The Queen pays no income tax. No one in the Royal Family has to pay income tax on Civil List money; but the Queen herself pays none at all, not on anything. Neither on the revenues she receives from the Duchy of Lancaster, nor on her own private fortune.

Apart from the Civil List money, the Queen receives about half a million pounds a year from the Duchy of Lancaster, and this is used for her Privy Purse money. This pays for clothes, robes, uniforms, pensions for her employees, and the upkeep of her private homes, Sandringham and Balmoral.

I never felt this left a great deal that she had to spend from her private money, which, it is said, must run into tens of millions. What else does she have to spend it on, except horses and racing, and breeding dogs? And the number of her possessions is astronomical, too. All the jewelry, with the exception of the Crown Jewels on display at the Tower of London, belongs to her personally. The Queen also owns Ascot Racecourse. The profits—which must be considerable —go into the Privy Purse: the reason, no doubt, why the Royal racing week is held at this course.

The Queen also owns property and investments, has bank accounts, and receives the best financial advice possible. It seems ridiculous that the Royal Family should be so penny-pinching, though the Queen is forever facing criticism from Britain's antimonarchist faction and tries to avoid anything ostentatious.

Not appearing rich is very much on all their minds. When Prince Charles's Aston Martin had to be serviced, Mr. Terry, who deals with the Royal cars, sent a Rolls-Royce to fill in. When Prince Charles came downstairs to leave the Palace for his midweek polo, he was furious.

"What's this?" he said.

"It's the replacement car, sir," I told him. He had to use it, because we hadn't anything else, but he was very reluctant to be seen in it. "Bad for the image," he said.

The Queen is generous with her Privy Purse when it comes to helping out those members of the family who either have small Civil List allowances or none at all. Her cousin, Prince Michael of Kent, lives extravagantly and has a foreign wife who yearns to be on the Civil List, but, as I have already explained, second sons (apart from those of the Monarch) are not and never will be. Prince Michael of Kent

ROYAL PENNY-PINCHING AND FINANCES

has to earn money, in spite of his position. That is not because the Royals do not approve of his wife; it is simply because of the rules. If worst came to worst, it is unlikely, however, that the Queen could ever permit a close relative to go broke. She would certainly have to bail him or her out.

When Princess Anne married, the Queen bought her a home, a fine manor house, Gatcombe Park. It cost £680,000. Though the Princess's husband, Captain Mark Phillips, is a successful farmer, it does not do for the Royal Family to appear too commercial. Therefore, the Queen does have to help them a little. But they are trying to increase the family budget. Captain Phillips's show-jumping is financed by the Range Rover firm. In August 1983 he opened the house for a two-day show-jumping and cross-country event. The plans are for this to become a regular summer money-raiser.

The Prince of Wales is not as rich as the Queen. He is not even on the Civil List, and will not be so until he becomes King. He and his Princess live on the money they receive from the Duchy of Cornwall. This is another trust, like that of the Duchy of Lancaster, owning land, property and investments. The land was mostly acquired by the Crown before the days of Henry VIII. In 1983, Prince Charles received £795,126 from this trust, but 25% went back to the taxman. If the Prince should die before becoming King, Princess Diana, as his widow, would receive £60,000 a year from the Civil List.

Just before the Royal wedding, Prince Charles was visited by his lawyers, Messrs. Farrar and Company, at Buckingham Palace. As they trooped into his study, Lady Diana (as she was then) came along to me in the waiting room and said, "Do you mind if I stay here with you for a few minutes?" She pulled a face and added, "He's doing The Will."

The Duke of Edinburgh is probably the most money-minded of them all. It is he who made Sandringham into a well-run estate that actually produces an income. Most of the Ribena (a British blackcurrant drink) is made from the blackcurrants grown at Sandringham. They keep and sell ducks. The dogs—corgis and Labradors—are bred there, and they too are a source of income. The staff are allowed to buy pheasants and apples from the estate at a cut rate, but nothing is given away. Also at Sandringham, which is on the East Anglian coast, the Duke is constantly reclaiming land from the sea. He has already created a few hundred acres to enlarge the estate.

Perhaps because so many people carp at the Royals about their finances, they hate people making money out of them. One day when we were at polo in Windsor, Prince Charles grumbled to one of the ever-present journalists, "I suppose you get paid extra for being here?"

"Your Highness," the journalist said patiently, "my pay packet at the end of the week won't change whether I'm here or somewhere else, or whether we publish a picture of you or we don't. It's just a job. It makes no difference to me."

The Prince looked totally unconvinced.

Having the Royal Warrant does not hurt, either. The warrant is, in fact, the Royal coat-of-arms, with BY APPOINTMENT TO HER MAJESTY THE QUEEN or whichever of the other three members of the family is permitted to give out warrants. Shops and businesses that serve the Queen, Prince Philip, the Queen Mother, and Prince Charles are given permission to display the warrant on their shopfronts, packaging, and even notepaper. Three years ago, there was great consternation when many old-established businesses were told to take their Royal Warrants down. Suddenly, one saw in the West End of London mysterious empty patches on the frontages of establishments like Trumper, the barbers, leaving gaps and shadows where the Royal Warrant used to hang.

I was responsible for the Prince's warrants, and I chose which shops he bought from. A little bit of bribery does go on. There is one famous clothing shop in Piccadilly—Simpson—which has had the Royal Warrant for years. I doubt if anyone from the Royal Family has ever bought anything there, but some members of the Household shop there all the time. Well, they would. They get a very advantageous rate.

Though it is quite difficult to get the warrant, I did manage it for a friend of mine when he worked at Asprey, probably the most famous shop in London. I just used to pop in and have things like the Prince's cufflinks repaired, or a piece of glass engraved. We certainly did not spend a lot of money there, but this doesn't count when applying for a Royal Warrant. All the shop has to do is prove it has been a Royal supplier for three years by sending in the receipts to prove it.

The Lord Chamberlain's office hands out the right to use the warrant, and it was the Lord Chamberlain who started the purge when so many were withdrawn. It was a sensible move, as the Royals wouldn't even have recognized some of the businesses that held the warrant if they drove by them. Still, Headlines (Princess Diana's hairdresser) will be eligible once she has been Princess of Wales for three years, and so, I suppose, will be a new batch of trendy dress designers.

The most deserving warrant is that given to Harrods, where most of the Royal shopping is done. This is where all the Queen's Christmas presents come from, year after year. They are brought to the Palace by Mr. Knight, who owns a gift shop in Surrey and who now goes shopping for her.

I'm afraid no American shop or organization holds the warrant. The Royals have to be seen to be buying British. They always drive British cars. A great supplier of these is Ford, which leases them to the family at favorable rates. Princess Margaret has been seen driving the new Mercedes 190, and the word is that she will get to keep it on "permanent loan." Permanent loan is the Royal way of getting around the problem of accepting commercial gifts.

Another way of accepting gifts is for "special occasions." Like the treasure trove of wedding presents that Prince

Charles received when he and Lady Diana married. And the astonishing collection of riches that were sent for the Queen's Silver Jubilee.

When Prince Charles was invested as the Prince of Wales, Harvey's of Bristol, a famous British wine firm, sent him hundreds of jeroboams of specially bottled sherry. A jeroboam holds four bottles' worth and is a magnificent sight. Each bottle was splendidly adorned with the Prince of Wales feathers and a label stating that it had been especially produced for the investiture. I still have one that the Prince gave me, and though the sherry is probably now undrinkable, I would not dream of parting with it.

But for all the time I was in Royal service, I never could quite believe their attitude to money. But then, they are not particularly familiar with the stuff. They don't even own credit cards; they don't need to.

They think the whole subject of money is rather vulgar—certainly new money. And yet they are fascinated by it. Prince Charles was always intrigued by people who had made a great deal of money by their own efforts; he was fascinated and yet slightly appalled at the same time. I remember being with him at a reception in the United States at which the guest list seemed to be wall-to-wall millionaires.

"Imagine," he said, "the wealth in this room could probably pay off the national debt." It never seemed to occur to him that the combined Royal Family's wealth could probably do exactly the same thing.

The truth is that they don't really understand money in the way we lesser mortals do. Normally, Prince Charles never sees a bill. His office takes care of all that, and though he grumbles about the price of things when paying for presents for the family at Christmas, he has no idea what things really cost.

I remember once when a bill crept by mistake into his personal post. He peered at it suspiciously and handed it to me. "What's this?" he asked.

ROYAL PENNY-PINCHING AND FINANCES

I inspected it and said, "It's a bill for hay, sir. For the polo ponies."

He took it back and looked at it again. "My God!" he said, aghast. "Do you realize that hay is forty pounds a ton! There's nothing else for it. I shall have to give up polo."

Well, he hasn't and he won't, until, as with the Duke of Edinburgh, the game gets too much for him. In the meantime he will continue to indulge himself with this rich man's sport and endeavor not to be aware of how much it is costing him.

But then he does only carry money once a week . . . on Sundays, to put in the church collection plate. When I was working for him, he always put in £1, and every Saturday night I would put the note on his dressing table, ready for the morning.

Prince Philip, who has less money than his son, thought that to give £1 was mean, and he was always saying so. The message got through. One Saturday night I found a note on Prince Charles's dressing table, saying, "Stephen, from now on make it £5." Then in a separate paragraph he had written "Inflation!"

On Sunday morning, he picked up the bank note I had left and turned it over, puzzled. "What's this?" he asked.

"A five-pound note, sir," I said.

It was the first he'd ever seen.

Chapter Nine

HER MAJESTY QUEEN ELIZABETH, THE QUEEN MOTHER

IF BY ANY CHANCE THE QUEEN MOTHER HAPPENED TO SAY IN the hearing of William, her steward, "What an unpleasant color this room is!" the chances are that he would pass on the word and the staff would stay up all night to repaint the offending walls a color nearer her taste. The Queen Mother's staff adore her; most of them have been with her for years. When retirement comes around for them, she will say, "I don't see why you should retire. I haven't."

And indeed, she has not. When she turned eighty-four in August 1984, she still undertook hundreds of engagements a year and never showed a trace of boredom. One of her little adages—of which she has many—is "Your work is the rent you pay for life."

Of all the Royals, her staff turnover is the lowest. Reginald, her page, has been with her for twenty-five years. A forthright Yorkshireman, he first came into Royal service when he worked as valet to the Duke of Windsor in Paris. Everyone likes Reginald. Princess Alexandra once described him as "someone who always gives an honest answer."

William, her devoted steward, has been with her for thirty years. He is a handsome, courteous man, and perfect for the job. She relies on him enormously. He runs the house for her, and even buys her Christmas presents for her.

Altogether, the Queen Mother employs about one hundred people including daily staff, but her main household consists of two Royal footmen, two household footmen, a chef, and two cooks. She retains the old-fashioned habit of calling her two dressers by their surnames. She has three chauffeurs, eight cars, and her own switchboard staff. She also employs the only female gardener in Royal service, a positive lady called Binny, whose pride and joy is the perfect lawn at Clarence House, the Queen Mother's London home.

Binny swears at anyone who dares set foot on the grass (with the exception of the Queen Mother). She was once heard to shout at Princess Alexandra, "Get off my bloody lawn!" Clarence House is in the Mall, which the Queen Mother calls "just down the road"—meaning, from Buckingham Palace. Attached by a covered way to St. James's Palace, Clarence House is itself very impressive. It was built for William IV in 1825, and will probably become Prince Charles's home one day.

One of the Queen Mother's other homes is Royal Lodge, in Windsor Great Park, and there she keeps a completely separate staff. Her under-butler at the lodge was old James Frost, who had been in service forever. People used to say, "How long have you worked for Royalty, James?" and he would reply solemnly, "I've boiled water for five queens."

The Queen Mother rather likes her staff to be characters. Another of her footmen (now no longer with us) always had Tuesday afternoons off. This was so that he could go to the Englefield Women's Institute meeting. He was the only male member of this nationwide women's organization. They had invited him to join because he created the most exquisite embroidery.

For many years, the Queen Mother was looked after by two dressers who sounded like a music hall act—Field and Suckling. Field and Suckling had their own dressers' dog, a plumpish dachshund called Pippin, who had started life as Princess Margaret's dog. Since Princess Margaret is not really fond of animals, Field and Suckling gradually acquired Pippin. Wherever they went, he went—and settled down very happily in the wardrobe department.

Although the Queen Mother now has two new young dressers who are really rather earnest by her standards, the two older ladies are still about, and will come in and help at busy times. Suckling is an absolute clone of the Queen Mother, having modeled herself upon her mistress. And—come to think of it at times she can be rather grander than her mistress.

Field is better remembered for being greedy. She adored her food and drink, and was always waiting for the next meal. She once amused the Queen Mother when she had one of those small disasters that the Royals love. Field was coming down some aircraft steps, following her mistress and carrying the Royal hat box when, unfortunately, the catch of this came undone. A bottle of gin fell out, landing on the tarmac, to be written off. Field was desolate.

Another of Field's little eccentricities was to pack up everything in sight when the Queen Mother was visiting away from home. Anything like fruit or biscuits or alcohol that had been left in the room for the Queen Mother's visit was packed up and taken off to Clarence House.

When traveling, the Queen Mother's staff, like the Palace

staff, is split. When staying at Birkhall (her home near Balmoral), she takes an indoor staff of seven or eight, compared with the one hundred twenty at Balmoral, a difference that causes a few grumbles.

Field used to travel with her more often than Suckling. But William, her steward, goes with her everywhere. He is indispensable as far as she is concerned. In the summer of 1983 he broke his arm, and couldn't go to Balmoral for the holidays. He was thrilled to receive a three-page letter from the Queen Mother, written on both sides of the page, wishing him well and asking why he didn't come up to Scotland, because the fresh air would do him good.

Michael Sealey, her chef, came to her from the Palace in a slight fit of pique when the Queen failed to recognize him— after seventeen years of service. There is no such danger with the Queen Mother. She is much closer to her staff, knowing how to get the best out of them by chat and personality.

Unlike the Queen, the Queen Mother sees her chef every day, so the menu-book is taken to her by Michael. She is quite a one for picking food that is costly or out of season. Asparagus and lobster, for example, are great favorites. But she will say, wheedling, having chosen something enormously expensive—like strawberries in December—"Oh, it's just a little treat, Michael."

"She has a little treat every bloody day," he says, shaking his head, half admiring, half disapproving, when he is back downstairs.

As it is, Clarence House is full of people looking after one lady. Though she upsets them occasionally, basically she can do no wrong. But one thing that can send her staff into a frenzy is that she can never make up her mind where she wants to eat lunch. She has a passion for eating in the open air, under the trees. But the climate is the governing factor as to whether or not this is possible. At eighty-four, she can't afford to take chances with catching a chill.

So, she looks out the window, sighs, and says to Reginald, "I think it had better be inside today. The weather looks uncertain." "Yes, Your Majesty," he says, and her staff lay up the table in her private dining room.

Then she will have another look at the sky and say, "Well, maybe it will be all right outside, after all." "Yes, Your Majesty," they say, and move everything outdoors and under the trees.

A quarter of an hour later, with her sweet smile and gentle manner, she suggests, "Do you think it is perhaps too cold?"

And back in again comes everything.

If you work for the Queen Mother, you quickly learn that she never actually says a positive yes or no, but just sails through a myriad of mind changes, or makes no decision at all. All with a smile that puts everyone on their knees to her.

I first encountered her charm when I stayed with the Prince at her home, Birkhall, in Aberdeenshire. The Prince loves getting away from the formality of Balmoral and into what he calls the "coziness" of his grandmother's house. Birkhall *is* lovely. The Queen Mother houses her fine collection of grandfather (long case) clocks in the big dining room, and the homely sound of their chimes punctuates the day.

What impressed me about her was that she came to greet me. Indeed, when we left she asked if everything had been all right. It may sound a simple courtesy, but it is not one that staff would normally expect from a Royal.

And her hospitality is amazingly generous. When she goes shooting at Balmoral, it's rather like joining Barnum and Bailey. She has a huge tent—getting on for the size of the Big Top. She is extremely fond of this tent, as it used to belong to her husband, the late King. Anything that was his, or that he liked particularly, is cherished to this day, even though he died in 1952. Her homes are all decorated in the colors he preferred; she has changed nothing of his.

But the tent, heavy and made of canvas, is a bit of an anachronism in this day and age. It weighs a ton, and the poor staff have to labor to get it up with the poles, pegs, and ropes. If the day is windy, they then have the problem of holding the thing down. This is generally done by parking the Land-Rovers on the corners, pinning the canvas with the wheels.

It is not always sufficient. One day Mum—as we irreverently called her behind her back—arrived to have lunch with her guests while the wind was blowing like billy-ho. The elegant luncheon party sat down inside, with the table laid with glass, silver, and fine china. The footmen were serving from silver trays while, outside, her steward and her chauffeur were desperately trying to hold the tent down.

I remember Prince Charles telling me that when his grandfather used to shoot at Sandringham, the head keeper had his own little tent, in which he did his own entertaining. One of the older keepers had told the Prince, who loves to hear stories of what he calls "the old days."

The Queen Mother keeps up many of the ways of the old days. She lives in grand style. At Clarence House she has a suite of offices for her Household, who are very close to her —so much so that it is quite usual for them to join her for meals when she is alone. That is something that rarely happens at Buckingham Palace. But then, "up the road" is stuffier than the Queen Mother's establishment.

Her Household numbers five senior male members: a treasurer, a chamberlain, a secretary, a press secretary, and a comptroller. Then there are four women: a Mistress of the Robes and three ladies-in-waiting.

The house has two comfortable drawing rooms which are used for receptions and small parties. When she gives a large party she will go "through the wall" into St. James's Palace. Clarence House has a cinema, but it hasn't been used for years. The Queen Mother prefers television, and will often have a meal on a tray while viewing.

At Balmoral and Sandringham she does watch films with

the rest of the Royal Family, instead of her beloved TV. One year, when the Royal film was *The Prime of Miss Jean Brodie*, the presenters cut out a scene which contained a Leonardo da Vinci drawing of a nude male. The drawing left little to the imagination, and they felt they should spare the Queen Mother's blushes. But she asked for the unexpurgated version to be shown at Balmoral, just to find out what she had missed.

Her tastes in entertainment are catholic. And her husband, the late King, loved a bawdy North Country comedian called George Formby. He liked him so much that Formby and his wife, Beryl, were frequently invited to the Palace to entertain. One evening the couple was leaving when Beryl fell over a rug. Solicitous as ever, the Queen Mother picked her up. Beryl Formby said cheerfully, "Don't worry, ma'am; where I come from, it's good luck. It means we'll be asked back."

"Oh really?" said Queen Elizabeth. "Well, you know where we live."

There isn't the faintest trace of snobbery about her, a trait that she has passed on to her daughter the Queen and her grandson Prince Charles. Her ease of manner with dustmen and Dukes probably goes back to her faintly eccentric father, the Earl of Strathmore, who, like his daughter, was someone with no airs but many graces.

An old story tells how he was gardening at their family home on a Sunday morning during the First World War. He was dressed—as the British aristocracy is wont to do on Sundays—in his oldest clothes. At the time his home was being used as a recuperation center for wounded soldiers. One of the soldiers, wandering in the gardens, stopped and watched him working for a while. Then he said, "Your boss, the Earl, must be a miserable old bugger to make you work on a Sunday."

"He is, rather," the Earl is reputed to have said.

HER MAJESTY QUEEN ELIZABETH, THE QUEEN MOTHER

The Queen Mother is truly her father's daughter. Off duty she has the most amazing collection of terrible old clothes that she uses for gardening, fishing, and walking.

Public appearances are a different matter. In her dressing room (which looks out over the Mall) the walls are lined with closets full of the highly exotic, furred and feathered clothing she loves. On top of the closets are rows and rows of hat-stands where her sometimes bizarre hats are placed.

When she is dressed, no one could look more like a queen. For her the crinoline has never gone out of fashion, and she has been described affectionately by her subjects as a cross between a Christmas tree, Nelly Wallace (an old-time music hall star), and the cockney "pearly queen." She always carries huge, floppy purses that match her dresses. These are made by Ivy Fields, her former dresser. When the Queen Mother has a dress made, she asks for an extra yard of the material, and Ivy runs up these rather strange, enormous handbags.

She always looks wonderful, regardless. One of the perks she gives her senior staff is to let them bring their families to Clarence House when she is going out, dressed to the nines, for some official function. It is a marvelous treat for "mums" and "aunties" to stand at the foot of the grand staircase as she sails through, saying a few words, and glittering from tiara to toe.

Reginald, her page, is of the opinion that she is just prac-ticing for the few gracious words she will be saying later at whichever function she is attending. But visitors are warned never to discuss her age or how well she looks.

She is rarely seen in the evenings without a tiara, which she keeps on with a small hairpiece. In her eighties, her hair is now a little thin. It is so unusual for her not to wear a tiara that she unwittingly embarrassed the organizer of a musical evening at St. James's Palace. To get into St. James's Palace from Clarence House, we used to go through "the hole in the wall" where the two buildings join. On this occasion, the Queen Mother went through, closely followed by her lady-in-waiting. The Chairwoman was waiting to greet her, wearing a magnificent tiara. When she rose from her curtsy, she saw the Queen Mother eyeing her hard—Her Majesty had left hers back home in her jewel box. . . .

Having got over the shock of upstaging Her Majesty, the poor woman then noticed that pattering behind her Royal guest were two corgis. "Oh, Your Majesty; your dogs have come through," she said.

The Queen Mother smiled sweetly. "They'll be all right," she said. "They're very musical, you know."

Like all Royals, she does have the odd blind spot about the staff. During the summer months, while the Royal Family are at Balmoral, all the overhaul work to the Royal residences is put in hand by the Department of the Environment. This can mean major or minor repairs. At Clarence House, the linoleum was worn through to a thread where the corridors come through into the servants' quarters from the main part of the house. The Queen Mother was checking the work that needed doing with the man from the Department, and he suggested that perhaps it would be a good idea to replace this linoleum with carpet tiles.

"They wear very well, and are easily replaced," he explained.

On being informed of the cost, the Queen Mother thought for a moment and then said, shaking her head, "No, I don't think so. I know they like their lino." Her staff are still puzzled as to what gave her that idea, and they still have their chilly "lino"—albeit, newer—on the floors.

These small, mean economies persist throughout the Royal Family, though the Queen Mother is less guilty than most. It is a family tradition that, at some anniversaries, they give the staff an extra little present. Not money, but cufflinks or something to keep. And they generally have some small gift on hand for a spontaneous gesture of this kind.

The Queen Mother gives the most generous Ghillies' Ball

every summer at Balmoral, and the Jack Sinclair Band from Glasgow have played for it year after year. The Queen Mother does not like change, so every year it's the same band, the same tunes, the same dances, and the same Queen. One summer Jack Sinclair reminded William, "Tell Her Majesty that this is my thirtieth year here, will you?"

"All right," said William, but, being busy, he promptly forgot all about it.

As usual the ball began at ten and the Queen Mother danced with as many of her guests as was possible until the midnight interval when late supper was served. She herself never stays until the end, but likes the dance to go on. She believes, quite rightly, that her guests don't really relax until she leaves, at which point the liquor really flows.

But before she departs, her routine is to go to where Jack Sinclair stands on the stage, and say, "Thank you so much, Mr. Sinclair. You won't mind playing on to the end, will you?" And he always says, "Oh, of course not, ma'am."

This particular year he said his piece and waited, expecting the floppy purse to open and a pair of cufflinks to appear. But—nothing. Quickly, he said, "Do you know, Your Majesty, this is my thirtieth year playing for you?"

"Really?" she said, giving him her gentle smile, and nothing else. "How time flies! To think that next year will be your thirty-first." And off she sailed.

She does have a nice sense of humor. One of the footmen was convulsed with laughter after attending a lunch among her, Princess Margaret, and the Queen. It was out of the ordinary for them to join one another for a meal when in London, and the Queen suddenly said—also unusual for her—"Do you know? I think I shall have another glass of wine."

"Should you, Lillibet dear?" asked the Queen Mother gravely. "You do have to reign all afternoon."

Another footman, riding on the back of the Queen Mother's coach at the Royal Show, passed this one on: It was a windy day, and the Queen Mother, visiting the big yearly agricultural event, was sharing an open carriage with Sir Dudley Forwood, the honorary director.

The footman could see that Sir Dudley was terrified that the Queen Mother's hat was going to blow off. His hand kept twitching towards the brim at every gust of wind. Finally he could bear it no longer. He put his hand firmly on her head to anchor the feathered creation down.

The Queen Mother was charmed.

"Oh, Sir Dudley," she said. "In a more gracious age I would have made you my Comptroller of Hats."

It isn't surprising she is loved. "It's made to doctor's orders," she says about anything that pleases her. Or, "This is a treasure." About the only thing that anyone could criticize her for is her constant unpunctuality, and this is something she has been fighting all her life. Her dressers go mad trying to get her together for her public engagements.

She is equally unreliable when it comes to time with her family. The Queen and Prince Philip like to dine at 8:15 when they are at Balmoral and Sandringham. The Queen Mother was always late; so they gave up and changed the time of dinner to 8:30. She still frequently runs late.

The Queen Mother must be the only guest who need not consult the table plan for her seat. Where she is placed is immediately obvious. She always sits in her own special chair, a fine carver with arms. She has a footstool placed underneath; and her own private thermos flask, full of ice, is on the table beside her place setting, ready to cool her champagne. It is one of her "little treats" to have a glass of champagne after dinner. She is almost invariably the only person at table drinking champagne, as the Queen does not serve this wine with dinner.

Protocol goes out of the window when she is dining with her daughter. She is always served before the Monarch.

Even as a young girl, the Queen Mother was always unpunctual. Fortunately, her father-in-law, the late King

George V, adored her. A stickler for punctuality himself, he expected everyone to be the same. If lunch was at one, he meant one, and everybody had to be in their places at table as the clock struck. Nothing infuriated him more than a guest arriving late for a meal when he was already seated.

This story is, of course, Palace history, as I most certainly wasn't around at the time. Apparently on one of the first occasions that the new Duchess of York (as the Queen Mother was after her marriage) had lunch with her in-laws, she was two minutes late.

She arrived, flustered and anxious. The King said gallantly as she made her apologies, "No, no, you are not late, my dear. It is we who are early." Those at the table couldn't believe their ears.

George V also wrote to his son five months after the wedding, "The more I see of your dear little wife, the more charming I think she is, and everyone falls in love with her here." They called her "The Smiling Duchess" in those days. Years later she would be called "Her Maternal Majesty."

Probably the only thing she disliked about the role fate had thrust on her was that, unlike Princess Diana today, she had to leave her children behind when she went abroad on Royal tours. It was, of course, tougher then on the Queen Mother, because every trip took so long. At least these days, flying makes any trip that much shorter.

The first tour the Queen Mother undertook was to Australia when her elder daughter, Elizabeth, was just eight months old. The King and Queen went by ship. Away for six months, she wrote to her mother-in-law, the old Queen Mary: "I felt very much leaving. The baby was so sweet, playing with the buttons on Bertie's uniform, that it quite broke me up."

If I sound as if I'm eulogizing the lady, it is because she has always enchanted people. Her husband, King George VI, wrote to the present Queen, "Mummy, as you know, is the most marvelous person in the world in my eyes." And until Princess Diana came along, she was the most wonderful person in the world in Prince Charles's eyes. She and his great-uncle, Lord Louis Mountbatten, were the greatest influences on him—Lord Louis for advice, the Queen Mother for sheer love.

She was very much an ordinary Granny to Prince Charles. She would bathe him and Princess Anne and put them to bed when their parents were away on official duties. The Prince cut his teeth on an ivory-handled rattle that had once been the Queen's and that his grandmother had put away for her grandchildren. It was passed to Princess Anne's son, Peter. I'm told that Prince William has it now, making three generations of Monarchs who have happily waved and chewed on it.

The Queen Mother also taught Prince Charles to fish, which has been an abiding pleasure for him. Until recently, it was still an abiding pleasure for her. Even at eighty she would wade out up to her thighs in the middle of a rushing salmon river, giving her staff palpitations. The Prince's favorite fishing place is still that stretch of the River Dee which runs through the Queen Mother's Birkhall estate.

It is my belief that it will be the Queen Mother's wish that Birkhall should go eventually to her favorite grandson. My feelings about this were confirmed when, only three years ago, she spent over £100,000 renovating the kitchens and the dining room in the house. For a lady in her mid-eighties, she is obviously planning a future for her home.

The house has the most beautiful gardens, and, though the Queen Mother flies no standard at Birkhall, it is obviously her home. Coming up the hill, one of the first things to catch the visitor's eye is the Queen Mother's cypher, picked out in lucky white heather on a grassy bank. All the Royals love gardens, but most don't get their hands dirty. When Prince Charles was five, the Queen Mother bought him a set of gardening tools, and with him it "took." Now that he has his own home, Highgrove, he loves pottering around. What he learned as a child has developed into a keen interest, and he has created his own garden.

The Queen Mother had Prince Charles with her at Birkhall many times during his childhood, when the Queen and the Duke were on Royal tours. When he went to school at Gordonstoun and was so unhappy, it was to his Granny he turned. He told me he had planned to run away to Birkhall. "I was going to hide in the woods," he said.

What he did was to write a sad letter to his grandmother, asking if she could rescue him from Gordonstoun. The Queen Mother literally put on her hat and coat and went to reassure him. She made him feel that it wouldn't be long before he could come to Birkhall again.

For, as much as she loves Prince Charles, she would never have discouraged him from doing what she would feel to be his duty. In spite of her easy manner, she is a staunch upholder of the Monarchy, and believes that things must be done properly.

Some of the more modern aspects of Royalty do throw her. When the Queen's accountant Edward Groves retired in 1983, the Queen saw fit to give him a knighthood. Something went wrong and the Queen Mother was not informed of the honor.

On the day he was leaving, William showed him into her private sitting room. She had planned to say goodbye, and to give him a small present and a signed photograph of herself, as he had done some work for her.

"Sir Edward Groves, Your Majesty," William said as he ushered him into the room.

The Queen Mother did a distinct double take, and for a moment was definitely thrown. There on her desk in front of her was the picture, signed to "Mr. Groves." Being very correct about these things, she gave him the present and then sent the photograph on later, as if it had been an extra thought.

It is not only Prince Charles who gains support from her.

She is also close to Princess Margaret and has steadfastly supported her throughout her daughter's stormy life.

"Clarence House was like one of those weather man-and-woman gadgets," one of the Queen Mother's staff said at the time of the Princess's marriage breakup. "Lord Snowdon coming in one door to discuss the problem with 'Mum,' and the Princess going out another."

The Queen Mother was fond of Lord Snowdon—she still is, in fact, and was sympathetic to them both. After the marriage was over, it was the Queen Mother who waived all protocol and had the Princess's new love, Roddy Llewellyn, the son of a millionaire show-jumping knight, to stay for weekends at Royal Lodge.

Probably the only time in her life that she has publicly broken—rather than bent—the Royal rules was on her eightieth birthday. She arrived last and left first for the service of thanksgiving at St. Paul's Cathedral—upstaging the Monarch. But she did so by special decree of the Monarch, her daughter. For the first time since she became Queen in 1952, she took a back seat to her mother. And what a day that was.

After the service at St. Paul's, the Queen turned to her and asked, "Well, Mummy, did you enjoy that?"

"Oh, so much, dear," said the Queen Mother. "Now I feel as if I can go on to be a hundred."

It just happens that one of the Queen's duties as Monarch is to send greeting telegrams to any of her subjects reaching their centenaries. At her mother's remark, she pulled a wry face and said, "In that case I think you'll have to get Charles to send the telegram. I doubt if I'll be around."

Prince Charles presented his grandmother with a portrait of herself in soft crayon, which he had specially commissioned. Usually it was I who would telephone William for suggestions on what to buy at Christmas and birthdays, but this time the Prince thought of it for himself.

The birthdays of Her Majesty Queen Elizabeth, the Queen

Mother, are always something of an occasion. From the early morning of August 8, the crowds start to gather outside Clarence House, ribbing the sentries in good-humored fashion. At some point the Guards march past on their way to Buckingham Palace for the Changing of the Guard, and as they go by they always play "Happy Birthday to You," and the spectators all sing lustily.

The Queen Mother eventually appears on her balcony. But she is so little that the staff have to put a small pair of steps, like a box, up there for her to stand on. Otherwise, no one could see her. The box elevates her above the geraniums that edge the balcony.

At 2:30 P.M. the large gates of Clarence House are opened, and the Queen Mother, accompanied by her daughters and any grandchildren who happen to be in London, comes onto the sidewalk to acknowledge the crowds and receive flowers. Then they all smile and wave before going back, and everyone is delighted.

It is a good day for the staff, too. Wine is served to everyone, and the Queen Mother's health is toasted. The atmosphere is terrific.

Her eighty-second birthday was particularly important. She shared it with Prince William, who was christened that day. And so this remarkable woman who, as the Archbishop of Canterbury said, "shows the human face of Royalty," has lived to see the future of the Monarchy projected into the twenty-first century.

Another time when the Queen Mother joins her staff is at Christmas. She always visits the stewards' room and the staff dining room—where one hundred people in all are celebrating with Christmas lunch—to watch turkeys being carved, and to wish everyone a happy Christmas, before going upstairs for her own meal.

Though she was born in the reign of Queen Victoria, there is little that is stuffy about the Queen Mother. She has a passion for racing, and everyone is aware that she has a string of racehorses, trained for her by Fulke Walwyn, and also by Bob Champion, an ex-jockey who triumphed over cancer.

She reads the *Sporting Life* avidly. When a British jockey called Terry Biddlecombe appeared on the TV program *This Is Your Life*, to his astonishment she sent him a telegram of congratulation. Royalty are not supposed to bet. I can reveal that the Queen Mother does have the odd flutter. She has a "blower" in her home, a private broadcast network that gives out racing information and betting prices.

She can't resist the thrill of the occasional bet. When she is in Canada, she will give one of the Royal aides a pound or two to put on a horse. If it loses, the subject is never mentioned again. If it wins, he has instructions to give the money to her favorite Canadian hospital. The Queen Mother's knowledge of racing is immense. We staff have long suspected that she wins a good deal more than she loses.

Another aspect of her character that makes her loved is that she is careful not to embarrass people. And that is something you can't say for all the Royals. Some of them enjoy a laugh at other people's discomfiture.

Like everyone else in the family, the Queen Mother never goes anywhere without a detective. When the Royals are at a private engagement, often the detectives are left kicking their heels until it is time to go home. So they usually find themselves sitting in someone's kitchen, and they are generally given a drink or two.

On one night the Queen Mother set off for home with her detective. It was a Friday, and she was going to Royal Lodge. As the car nosed its way through the heavy London traffic her detective, sitting in the front passenger seat, gently dozed off. Suddenly, the chauffeur stopped the car with a jerk, to avoid going through traffic lights. Startled, the detective woke up, and with a complete reflex action, he leaped out of the car, opened the rear door, and stood waiting for the Queen Mother to emerge.

She leaned forward so she could look up at him. "Shouldn't we go a little further?" she suggested. "To Royal Lodge, perhaps?"

Only then did the still faintly woozy detective look around him. The car was stationary right in the middle of Hammersmith Broadway, one of the less salubrious areas of London. Red in the face and desperately embarrassed, he shut the Queen Mother's door and shot back into the car himself.

"She never said another word," he said afterwards, telling the story on himself.

I personally witnessed one of the funniest Queen Mother incidents ever. It happened when Prince Charles was dreaming of buying the new Rolls-Royce Camargue, a magnificent sports model. The Royals have a Mr. Terry who buys cars for both the Household and the family. The Prince had asked if he would bring a test model of the Rolls down to Royal Lodge one Sunday morning after church, so that he could try it out. The Prince was staying with his grandmother, and I was deputed to look out for the car's arrival.

It duly appeared, driven by Mr. Terry, who parked it outside the Queen Mother's home, where it sat looking for all the world like something out of a catalogue. The Prince was held up, talking to some people outside the church, and the Queen Mother arrived home before him. The first thing she saw was this splendid car parked on her drive, with Mr. Terry leaning nonchalantly on the hood. As he straightened up and bowed, she said, "Good morning, Mr. Terry; how are you?" Then added, "And what is this?"

"It's a Rolls-Royce, Your Majesty," Mr. Terry said, his voice reverent. "The latest model. I brought it for Prince Charles to look at."

"Indeed?" she said, moving slowly round it. "It is very fine, isn't it?"

"It is. It is," he said, then asked diffidently, "Would you like to try it, ma'am?"

Without hesitation she said, "How kind!" and made her

way to the car, standing waiting for the door to be opened. Mr. Terry leaped to oblige. And then she noticed his tipping the front seat forward so that she could climb into the back.

It was probably the first time in her life that the Queen Mother had been confronted by a two-door car. She looked faintly puzzled for a moment; then without missing a beat, she smiled her sweetest smile and murmured, "Perhaps another time, Mr. Terry, another time . . ." and turned to walk into the house.

I was hovering, waiting for the Prince, and I'm afraid I was almost crying with laughter once she was out of sight. But it took a moment for Mr. Terry to realize that the prospect of climbing into the back seat was what had made her change her mind. The Prince never bought the car, though he yearned for it. He was afraid it would look as if he were being extravagant.

It is said that when the Queen Mother was only a small girl she wrote in an autograph book that her favorite pastime was making friends.

She has done that all her life.

This again is history—long before my time at the Palace but I think it is worth repeating here. After the King died, she was left a widow at the age of fifty-two. She said to the British nation of her husband: "He loved you all. Every one of you. That was the pledge he took at his Coronation. Now I am left to do what I can to honor that pledge without him."

That pledge she has honored magnificently.

HER MAJESTY QUEEN ELIZABETH, THE QUEEN MOTHER

ABOUT THE AUTHOR

Stephen P. Barry came into the Palace as a footman in 1967 at the age of eighteen. Only three years later he found himself traveling around the world with Prince Charles, organizing the incredibly busy workload of the future Monarch. He left Royal service shortly after the Prince's marriage, when it became evident that Princess Diana wanted her husband to make a clean break with his bachelor days. Stephen Barry wrote of his experiences in *Royal Service*, which was an international best-seller. He currently lives in London.